WAR

A Simple Guide to a Complex Phenomenon

By

John Plant

New Generation Publishing

Dedicated to the memory of
the 13th/18th Royal Hussars

Cover:
Dhofar, 1973

Contents

Preface

A preface gives the author an opportunity to comment on his work, and I will take advantage of this. I have been fascinated by the phenomenon of war since the age of about four. This fascination was fairly natural. I was born in 1945 and all the men of my Father's generation had been in the forces. It was impossible for any boy to hear them talking about their wartime experiences and not want to be a soldier, and that is one ambition I have fulfilled. More significantly their words sparked up in my mind a desire to understand war, and I'm still working at this.

In following up my interest in war I have read any number of books titled something like 'The Art of War', and yet not one of them has, in my view, properly covered the subject. So, about ten years ago, I decided to try to do this myself. The reader will decide how successful I have been.

Over the ten years I have tried to think everything through and give as full a picture as possible, but even so there is something missing, the something that answers the question 'how can people do it?' At the very bottom level the question becomes, 'how can people accept this level of cruelty?' In terms of the extremes of primary warfare – a term I explain in the Introduction – the answer is racial hatred and necessity, but in terms of secondary warfare I believe the answer lies in a particular aspect of human nature in that once a person has surrendered, he hates anyone who hasn't.

On the battlefield this is natural, the fact that anyone is still fighting is a comment on the lack of courage of anyone who has surrendered. But even in a peacetime army the soldiers, who have surrendered to military discipline, will affect a contempt for civilians even if they sometimes envy them. Propaganda is worse. Once anyone has surrendered to it, which is to say, has been won over by, or has found it expedient to accept, a set of beliefs, be they political or religious, he will hate anyone who hasn't. Then he will be capable of amazing cruelty to unbelievers and free-thinkers. odium theologicum. *Of course the difference between propaganda surrendered to, and beliefs sincerely held, can be a little difficult to define.*

This principle linking surrender and hate, I find, explains a lot.

I feel I should try to explain why I am trying to make my opinions available to the reading public. In part there can be little doubt that it is vanity publishing, but a large part of my decision is down to a long-held belief that if only everyone understood war and peace, politics and the way the world is run, then, not immediately but over a period of years, all our political and social problems would fade away. Perhaps this belief is silly and naïve, but surely everyone has a duty to try to understand, and perhaps this book will help.

This study, for good or bad, is entirely my own work. However it has been read through by two retired officers whose judgement I greatly respect. They would not thank me for publishing their names, but I wish to say how grateful I am for their comments.

JPP
Sheffield 2010

Introduction

Warfare is an endlessly complex social phenomenon. However as it is a single phenomenon its manifestations should fall into a definite pattern. If this is so then this pattern must be capable of including not only great campaigns, such as Normandy in 1944, but also the latest Al Qaeda atrocity.

Establishing this pattern and describing it, so that a place can be found in it for each individual conflict, will be a significant aid to the understanding of that conflict and of warfare in general. This will be attempted in this study.

The phenomenon of war exists because it is an essential aspect of human nature that it is not difficult to get young men to kill others, usually strangers, for reasons that they might not understand or find to be personally irrelevant. How this can happen is a question of basic anthropology. Humans lack the thick carapace of the tortoise and the near impenetrable skin of the pachyderm. They cannot seek refuge in flight as can a horse. Consequently, in the unremitting struggles of evolution they have been forced to be aggressive, and because of their physical limitations, they have had to form groups.

Human groups, particularly of young men, are naturally antagonistic to outsiders. The group members give their prime loyalty to the group, and the suffering of people outside the group will mean little to them. It will be seen that basic anthropology stands behind every idea expressed in the following pages.

In the study of war the first step is to define two terms: Primary and Secondary Warfare. These terms were once commonly used but have rather fallen out of fashion. They are, though, good ones and will be used here.

Primary Warfare is usually taken to refer to the wars of

prehistory, when peoples were migrating, usually under the incentive of starvation. The combatants were the entire community, and the losers were either wiped out or, at least, driven out. Normally the protagonists were of different levels of civilisation, and both sides were driven by necessity, and consequently, desperate. A modern equivalent of Primary Warfare may be the situation of people in a failed state where there has been a total breakdown of law and order and everyman's hand is raised against his neighbour under the necessity of survival, and life is *'nasty, brutish and short'*. Conversely the modern equivalent might be Nuclear Warfare.

This study will consider warfare from an essentially British point of view, and from that point of view primary warfare is not of great importance. But it must not be forgotten that there are large areas of the developing world where failed states exist and where primary warfare is endemic. In such places the ebb and flow of population are facilitated by large numbers of small scale actions employing edged weapons like pangas and, where possible, AK47s. These wars, usually in poverty stricken areas, though little reported and never producing real battles, will cause more death and suffering than all the secondary wars waged over the same period.

In primitive societies there has sometimes been an amelioration of the excesses of primary warfare through its ritualisation, and this ritualistic warfare was not aimed at the destruction of tribes or peoples but rather the maintenance of the balance between them. It was as likely to be a display of the young men's *machismo* as waged for any more concrete aims. However this only occurred in primitive societies and in some cases, it might be suspected, because that society was not making any progress towards civilisation.

When societies did make progress towards civilisation a kind of limited warfare called Secondary Warfare emerged, and this is the form of warfare usually seen in the developed modern world. It can be characterised as being intelligently directed sustained military operations. The intelligent direction and the sustained nature of the operations are what lift war above the anarchy of a street gang fight. War in the modern world is usually of the secondary type and for the remainder of this study 'War' will mean 'Secondary War' unless otherwise stated.

The existence of secondary warfare is dependent upon the existence of a society capable of fighting it. This social system must include the People, who will pay for the war and, usually, provide the soldiers; the Government which will organise the people, tax them and plan the war; and the armed forces that will do the fighting. Any society that does not have these three distinct constituent parts will fail in secondary warfare in the following ways:

If the government merges with the armed forces then the troops become just a branch of the civil service whose job it is to keep the government in power applying a kind of martial law. This society will not be able to wage a successful secondary war as its forces, having become little more than police, will not be competent to.

If the government is not distinct from the people, as with the tribal democracy of a primitive people, then any warfare embarked upon by that people will not be intelligently directed over a long period but will depend on public emotion and will inevitably tend to primary warfare, or fade away.

If the people merge with the armed forces the result is a militarisation of society. At a low level, for example a state whose army is made up entirely of reservists, the military effectiveness of the army will be low and decisions for its use will be democratic, the voters being the soldiers. At a high level of militarisation the society which will become better and better at secondary warfare. Unfortunately this will have a bad effect on the domestic policy of the state and will result in it only being able to support itself by aggressive warfare, and this will become progressively like primary warfare. Finally it will be defeated and no longer have the internal resilience to recover. The obvious example is Sparta.

However even when these three categories are distinct they interact at many levels and each will influence the actions of the other two.

A war occurs when one government wishes to force another to alter its behaviour in some way, and the other government, or some part of its society, resists. This causes a conflict that might start at a very low level, such as the making of speeches and the writing of diplomatic notes, but will grow in intensity if the root cause is not resolved. Finally one side, or both, will deploy troops to gain their ends. As can be seen the word 'Conflict' is used to describe the entire range of inter-government friction. 'War' describes the situation when the conflict has become so intense as to result in fighting. Consequently to understand war it is necessary to consider the full range of conflict.

It is easy to see the driving force of secondary warfare as governmental policy, but governmental policy must take into account the emotions and prejudices of the population, and these can be surprisingly strong. The positive side of such emotions may result in a wave of patriotism during a war and a great boost for the popularity of the government, as was seen in Great Britain during the Falklands War. The negative side, which is usually based on racial antagonism, may result in the war being unnecessarily brutal, as was the case in the war against Japan during the Second World War. The effects of public opinion on policy do not yield to meaningful generalisations, but they should never be ignored

It is possible to imagine a case thereby a government, and army, are fighting a totally unorganised and uncivilised enemy, that is to say one with no government that pressure can be brought against. This, in the modern world, will be rare but could happen as a result of a failed state. It would be an extreme example of Asymmetric Warfare, and will be considered later.

For a war, then, usually two governments in conflict are required. There may be, of course, many more but they would be allied to one or the other to produce two warring sides. It follows that the nature of war can be understood by considering:

How societies and governments are formed, and what are their characteristics,

What causes them to fight,

How they go about it.

These questions will be studied in the subsequent pages.

1

Social Structures

People naturally form groups. These groups may initially be based on family, tribe or race. As the society becomes more sophisticated so it becomes larger and, as the societies clash in the struggle for scarce resources, the largest and best organised survives.

No doubt as they wandered in the wilderness, the twelve tribes of Israel were usually more than a match for any individual tribe they met.

While in a primitive state of civilisation any warfare that peoples undertake will tend towards primary warfare. The Children of Israel demonstrated this by massacring all who got in their way. If the society is nomadic it is unlikely to progress beyond primary warfare.

However once the people settle down then inevitably some sort of social stratification will emerge as individuals exert their personal superiority then pass on their characteristics, wealth and social position to their children. As social classes emerge so a recognisable society will start to form with Government, People and Soldiers. Initially it may only be that the non-combatants provide food for the soldiers as they go away to fight, but such specialisation quickly appears. This will result in the emergence of secondary warfare.

Illustrations taken from Biblical history may be pursued further to show how a society can slip from primary to secondary warfare. As the twelve tribes settled down in Palestine so they formalised their arrangements for primary warfare, which, in their case, would be better called 'Holy War'. When a threat occurred some, seldom all, of the tribes were called out. When they met they became *'the people of God'*, and after some cleansing rituals they hurled themselves on their enemy with primary brutality. Then, the fighting over, and after further rituals, they went home, *'to your tents, O Israel'*.

As the tribes became more civilised so kings were appointed and a regular army formed. From then on two types of warfare existed, the limited warfare of the regular troops obeying the king's orders, and the Holy War of the mass of the population, which was only evoked in an emergency. As the international situation stabilised so Holy War faded away, leaving the kings with their regulars and the people to pay taxes.

This concept of two types of warfare was well understood in classical times. The Greeks and Romans each had at least two deities of war whose natures expressed this. The Greek Athene, Goddess of War and Wisdom, was a remarkably creation. She was incredibly clever in the arts of peace, hated war but was prepared to fight in a good cause and never forgot her war aims. Ares, on the other hand, loved war and destruction. He was fearsome in action, but could be defeated by Athene. The Romans had similar beliefs, naming the two deities Minerva and Mars.

An illustration of how this could work out in practice was given in India. The Hindus had developed the caste system which allowed only a small privileged elite the honour of bearing arms. This enabled the Hindu rulers to war among themselves and keep the lower castes down, but it only used a small fraction of the Hindu military potential and resulted in them being conquered by Muslims from the north. This disaster was followed by a period of tyrannical repression which was only ended when the Sikhs abolished the caste system and made each Sikh liable for military service. The Sikhs then drove the Muslims out, but unfortunately the Sikhs' rule turned out to be every bit as repressive as that of the Muslims had been.

As societies evolve there comes a stage when all the trends of race, history, language and geography come together to create what are usually called 'Nation States'. The 'Nation' part of this expression refers to the people, and the 'State' refers to the political and legal establishments. This study will use only the first part of this expression, though the word 'Country' is used when a more general term is needed.

When considering European countries it is easy to regard them as historically stable, but there are many cases for which this is not so. For example when Montenegro was forcibly absorbed into Yugoslavia in 1918 it seemed to be gone for good, but at the time of writing it is Yugoslavia which is gone and Montenegro lives on. There have been great changes and small ones. For over five centuries the Grand Duchy of Lithuania included vast areas of what are now Belarus and Ukraine, but by AD 1800 it had been reduced to approximately the small modern Lithuania, a process that cost many lives. Conversely the very small country of Carpatho-Ukraine came and went in 24 hours in 1939 and the event cost no lives. It is unwise to believe that modern national boundaries are permanent.

It is impossible to define what makes certain nations viable and others not so. France, for example, started the last millennium as solely the Ile-de-France, but steadily expanded taking in other independent states until it reached its current borders. As late as the 1880s only 20% of the population regarded French as their first language. Despite absorbing what were really foreign countries it is today a viable nation. Yugoslavia, on the other hand, failed. However, the concept of the viable nation is basic to understanding secondary warfare.

Along with the nation comes nationalism. This should be a simple concept but, as with so much in human affairs, is difficult to pin down. The growth of nationalism is often linked to the rise of the middle class, and, as horizontal confrontations with other countries tend to vindicate and reinforce the existing social structure, and as the middle class is sometimes seen as being a little insecure socially, this linkage is quite reasonable. Because of the pre-1914 growth in trade tariffs substantial sections of the population grew rich behind tariff walls, and the middle class dramatically increased in size. Nationalistic belligerence increased while the liberal dream of universal peace founded on free trade crumbled.

However the growth in nationalism can also be linked to the standardisation of the nation's official written language. In the second half of the 19th Century populations were becoming fully literate and governments and civil services were expanding so everyone began to feel a part of the nation via the national language. This was happening when the populations had endured immense changes due to industrialisation and the drift from the countryside to the towns. As centuries-old loyalties, based on the local communities, had been destroyed the people were glad to latch on to the new and comforting loyalty to the nation. This comforting feeling, however, was vulnerable in that there were foreigners who might upset it, particularly as they spoke a different language. This developed into a tendency to blame foreigners for pretty-well everything that went wrong, and to believe that most problems could be solved by fighting them. Consequently public opinion would usually back its government in any action against foreigners.

There can be little doubt that the introduction of conscription among industrialised nations resulted in a dramatic increase of nationalism. The army ceased to be the 'King's' or the 'Czar's', but became 'ours', and a source of pride via shared experience. Even in Great Britain, where conscription was not introduced until 1916, the same effect was achieved by the volunteer movement, and particularly those volunteers who fought in the Boer War.

Perhaps it is best to relate the growth of aggressive nationalism back to the principle linking surrender and hate, as described in the preface. As the state grew in power, and laws and police required a greater surrender to the norms of modern industrial life, so resulting frustrations were deflected onto foreigners. The converse is that the state that failed to evoke this surrender to its laws, and failed to reduce the personal freedom of its citizens, was apt to be destroyed by its more aggressive neighbours.

In most European countries nationalism reached a peak in the decade before the Great War, a period when people could feel very defensive about foreigners but yet could not travel overseas to draw their own conclusions. This will be considered in a later chapter, but it is worth noting that as nations become more democratic so popular nationalism becomes more racially based just at the time when economic inequalities are causing mass immigration. This will cause problems in the future.

Nations, providing they have sensible borders and that usually means along ethnic boundaries, have proven remarkably stable. However not all societies evolve into nations:

Some form within existing nations, these may be called 'Sub-National SocialStructures', and the common cause of one forming would be the existence of a sizeable   ethnic minority.

Some are absorbed by an expanding nation and fade away, or remain as sub-national social structures.

Some form, or remain, outside the network of nations. These may be called 'Extra-National   Social   Structures',   and examples include:

    The Knights Templar,
    The Old Man of the Mountains,
    Al Qaeda,
    The World Zionist Organisation.

It is no coincidence that these examples all originate in the

Middle East, where the structure of nations was, and is, less strong than in Europe.

There has been a sudden blossoming of extra-national social structures in the later years of the 20th century. Most notable among these were the large US and British banks and large oil companies (Big Oil). These companies are the basis of the phenomenon of Globalisation, the long term effects of which are still in doubt. The early years of the 21st century have seen a potentially more worrying phenomenon, the rise of the super-rich. These are individuals with personal incomes greater than those of some small countries. They have no nationality and no share holders and are as much above the law as they want to be. These trends make the future difficult to predict.

It can happen that one nation could conquer several others forming a government over and above theirs, or several countries could come together and agree to act under a super-national government. Examples of these cases include the USSR, Yugoslavia and the EU.

Probably the most important scenario is that similar sub-national social structures could form in several countries then establish links and together become an extra-national social structure. Finally, becoming more powerful, they become a super-national political force, and the national structure they sprang from becomes less important. This seems to be the current trend of Militant Islam.

Left to themselves peoples and governments evolve into recognisable modern nations. Unfortunately they seldom are left to themselves. The governing hierarchies, and to some extent the nations themselves, are perpetually in a state of flux, both sub-national and super-national governments continually forming and dissolving. The former due to groups, most commonly immigrants, deciding that they have a common interest that sets them apart from the rest of the nation, and the latter usually due to the ambitions and vanity of politicians.

If societies do form recognisable nations, with democratic governments, they will live in peace and be the hope of the world as history shows that such nations do not have wars with similar ones. It is a little early in world history to be certain why this should be true. It may be so because it is difficult to demonise the open society of a potential enemy and the free press would be a counter- balance to belligerent government propaganda. Alternatively it may be because a mature and well functioning democracy is the final stage of national development, and this will assume that the state has well defined borders and a roughly homogeneous population and will be financially viable. Consequently it will have little to gain by war, and two such states will have even less to gain by fighting each other.

The progress towards democracy is by no means inevitable. If the emerging democracy is not deep rooted and is faced by difficult circumstances it may appear to be unable to muster the firm decision making capacity required and will become vulnerable to being replaced by a dictatorship. This happened to the Weimar Republic. Similarly many colonial countries were set up with democratic constitutions on gaining independence. They quickly fell to military coups.

The world, then, should be slowly moving to be a patchwork of democratic countries. Unfortunately there are two main counter-currents:

sub-national societies with their governing hierarchies may be more dynamic, being more democratic and having greater participation of the people.

Super-national governments will have the full panoply of repression and control ready formed.

Consequently it can be seen that the structure of nations is not forever static but must be continually maintained by deliberate government policy.

The perpetual flux of governing hierarchies accounts for how they can get out of step with their societies. This should not happen in a perfect democracy, but the sad fact is that most people will allow anything for a quiet life, so the government gets away with it.

It also shows how each government may have relations vertically with other governments above or below it, and horizontally with other similar governments, particularly in the case of national governments. These horizontal and vertical governmental relationships are the basis of the two major types of wars, horizontal and vertical wars these being usually, but not always, national and internal wars.

The concept of horizontal governmental relationships should not be confused with the pre-1914 socialist concept of an international working class. This was the belief that workers in one country had more in common with workers in another that they had with people of other classes in their own. This fallacy was exposed when socialist calls for workers to boycott the Great War went unheeded, much to the chagrin of the socialist writers who seem to have had no understanding of patriotism and been blind to obvious facts. Working class people, like everyone else, can only have any political power if they place themselves under a government. The choice is simple, to cling to the national government or to a trades union committee, or something similar. It is not surprising that they chose the national government. Without the organising and coercing power of a government, individuals can do little. They might manage a riot, nothing more.

The relationship between a government and its people may to some extent affect that government's propensity for aggressive warfare. In this context there are three basic types of government/people relationships:

Democracy, in which the people control the government.
Nationalist dictatorship, in which the government, though autocratic, actually has limited powers of coercion over the people.
Socialist dictatorship, in which the government has wide powers of coercion.

These are admittedly imprecise terms, but there do not seem to be any generally agreed alternatives. In fact various politicians and political commentators will tie themselves in verbal knots trying to think some up, and terms like 'Fascism' ultimately only serve to mislead. So, for the purposes of this study, a socialist dictatorship will have come to power by exploiting class antagonisms and will aim at restructuring society. A nationalist dictatorship will have exploited the existing social system. However the end results of both cases will be progressively similar as the governments, and governing classes, make changes to make themselves more secure and comfortable.

These three categories tend to affect aggressive horizontal, or national, warfare in different ways.

The first one, democracy, may allow a protracted defensive war, but will quickly veto an apparently aggressive one, as the US experience in Vietnam showed. Less obviously, any tension between the classes in a democracy may hinder the government's military plans. An example of this was given by Britain in the 1930s. The country was slow to rearm in the face of German militarism, and one reason for this was that the Labour party believed that the government had some kind of secret agenda to use troops against the working class, as almost happened during the general strike of 1926, so it remained pacifist until the Spanish Civil War started in 1936.

The second, Nationalist dictatorship, seems the most likely to result in aggressive warfare. Apart from any material gain the war, if successful, will distract the people from any grievance they might have with the government, and substantially improve the government's popularity.

The last, Socialist dictatorship, has, so far, resulted in little aggressive war as the governments have been fully occupied in repressing their populations. Perpetual revolution indeed!

The situation for vertical, or internal, warfare is slightly different.

In a democracy there will be no cause for internal warfare.

In both types of dictatorship governmental mismanagement results in discontent which cannot be dispelled in an election and, if not mollified will ultimately result in some kind of revolt. Generalisations are difficult but it seems that nationalist dictatorships are more likely to evoke *coups d'état*, and socialist dictatorships, uprisings. These are no bad things if they result in more democratic societies, but history shows that this is not particularly likely.

Put more succinctly, in a Nationalist context there is a tendency to try to solve problems by fighting other nations. In a Socialist context there is a tendency to try to solve problems by fighting a different social class.

Almost inevitably these neat classifications do not seem that obvious in the real world. This was shown in 2007 when the Palestinians voted in Hamas to replace Fatah. The latter group had kept the anti-Israel flame burning many years but were getting a reputation for *laissez faire* corruption and their anti-Israel actions seemed to be becoming less effective. Consequently the people decided they preferred the Islamic militancy of Hamas who, like socialists, will devote most of their energies to forcing their beliefs onto the people and have less time to deal with their foreign enemies. The result may well turn out to be explicable in the above terms, but not predictable.

2

Armies

Societies in their primitive state are only capable of primary warfare in which the army and people are the same thing. However, as they become more civilised so they develop a capacity for secondary warfare and the army becomes separate from the people. The process of civilisation involves the emergence of separate classes and the society's capacity for secondary warfare varies as the relationships between the classes, governments and people, change. As societies develop so their armed forces pass through a series of key stages.

1) Aristocratic

This phase is characterised by the emergence of a ruling class whose members are the only ones who can afford the quality weapons and have the skill to use them. Naturally they dominate their society, and the government and army can be said to have merged. In this phase   the   society   is capable of two distinct types of warfare. The population in general will still be able to wage primary war, but the aristocrats, when they are fighting aristocrats of another society, will fight in a ritualistic way developing ultimately into what could be regarded as chivalry. Providing there are no great shifts of population or technology, the aristocratic system will remain the norm until democratic pressure forces a change.

It will be natural for the aristocrats to discourage the population from indulging in primary warfare because it may result in a social upheaval that could threaten their position. This may leave the society vulnerable if in conflict with a people that does resort to primary warfare.

2) Militia

As the society expands there comes a phase when the contribution of the people, or at least the better off classes, is needed to provide larger armies. This results in the creation of a militia and a degree of democracy, no mater how limited, being forced on the government. This was the significance of the Roman crest SPQR, *Senatus Populusque Romanus*, the Roman Senate and People.

However, because of the part-time nature of these soldiers, democratic warfare is developmentally static and will tend either to degenerate into primary warfare or to fade away. Democratic societies always have difficulty in sustaining lengthy military operations. As the state becomes more sophisticated and the citizens prefer to get on with earning their living and not marching off to war, so the next phase emerges.

3) Professional

With the increasing difficulty of warfare comes the need for better trained soldiers. The government is now in a position to tax the people and pay soldiers. The soldiers may be regulars, or mercenaries, or even conscripts the principle is the same, they now obey the government. The militia, being a part of the people could put things to the vote, but this has now changed and the government is now fully in control, if less democratic. It can now use secondary warfare as a method of enforcing its policy in a sustained and calculated way impossible in the two earlier phases.

However the more an army depends on conscription the more the deployment of the armed forces must meet with the broad approval of the people. This is one reason why conscript armies do not defend governments against a revolution. Providing the government behaves sensibly the principle of military subordination to the civil government will obtain and will be very important.

The introduction of conscription might seen to be a democratic measure, but actually it has turned out to be the opposite. It has given governments greater opportunities to control and educate, or indoctrinate, the people.

The armed forces of all societies will pass through these phases, obviously so for nations, in other cases less obviously, providing only that the society involved continues to develop and is not adsorbed by another. If, however, a super-national government is created then its armed forces will spring into existence already formed in the professional stage.

In an attempt to clarify how a small, embryonic, sub-national social structure might pass through these phases, it is useful to consider the actions against the national government it might be involved in.

A *Coup d'état*

The society may be in the aristocratic phase even if the members of its governing hierarchy might decry the use of that expression. They could be the only ones capable of carrying out the attempt. There would be very limited mass action.

A Rebellion or Uprising

This will involve the militia stage, a large degree of mass action. But, providing the national government does not lose its nerve, or the loyalty of its armed forces, the weakness of a militia will soon be apparent.

A Revolutionary War

The purpose of the revolutionary governing hierarchy will be to achieve the professional stage as soon as possible and embark upon conventional operations, which is to say organised and uniformed armies fighting another such. In this case a civil war.

However all armies, even when they have reached the professional stage, are to some extent unique. This is because armies have several functions and each government will place a differing emphasis on each of these. Armies provide the pomp and ceremonial which are so good for political prestige. They provide the muscle behind the police forces, thereby maintaining stability and security for the government. If they are manned by conscripts the continual through-put of recruits enables education to be undertaken to improve national homogeneity. Armies are often unnecessarily large, this being good for national prestige and hence for the government's prestige. Also they can fight other armies.

In this study the armed forces discussed will usually be armies. Navies are subject to the same pressures as are armies but their activities are much more limited and technical in nature. So naval warfare will not be considered separately.

Each army will consider the range of operations it may be involved in, eg internal security, counter-guerrilla, conventional and nuclear warfare, then it will train for the highest form of operations among these. This, in general, is quite reasonable as an army that can handle the complexities of conventional warfare should easily handle internal security operations. However it can happen that heavily armed conventional troops are helpless in the face of guerrillas, or even a protesting crowd. Taken to an extreme a nuclear bomb is just not a credible weapon to deploy against a terrorist cell. One of the most famous images of the 1980s was a Chinese civilian, who presumably had been to the shops as he was carrying some shopping bags, banging on the glacis of a tank at Tiananmen square.

Probably the great difference between levels of warfare is the level of destruction involved. Too much destruction at a lower level of warfare is usually counter-productive and will reflect adversely on the government, as the Tiananmen incident was to show. The varying levels of destruction can be illustrated by urban warfare. At the highest end of the scale was the Battle of Berlin. This saw the total destruction of the city. This can be compared with urban fighting in Northern Ireland where the householder's rights were scrupulously respected.

Further, specialising in one type of warfare can blunt an army's edge for other types. For example the British Indian army between the world wars was very skilled in border hill warfare. This expertise did not help it in the jungles of Burma. These things must be carefully considered when structuring, arming and training an army.

Fully developed armies consist of Officers and Other Ranks. The Other Rank (OR) expression is now out of favour in the British army, but no really convincing alternative has been found. The difference between the two groups, put at the most simple level, is that the officers do the thinking and the ordering, and the ORs do the work and the fighting. The quality of an army's officers is the crucial measure of the quality of that army. Appendix 1, though flippant in style, gives a fair idea of the structure of the British army.

It is natural, and very necessary, that there is a wide gulf between officers and ORs. If this were not so military discipline would be difficult to maintain and officers could hardly make dispassionate plans for actions which might result in the deaths of many of their men. In the Red Army between the world wars, for doctrinaire reasons, this gulf was minimalised and some of the officers' functions were taken over by Commissars. After the German invasion of 1941 military necessity reasserted itself and officers' privileges and badges of rank reappeared and the commissars were downgraded.

The selection of officers is very important. There is simply too much to learn for officers to enlist as privates and work their way up through the ranks. Even if this were not true such a method might result in the officers having too much sympathy for the ORs and a resulting risk of poor discipline. Therefore the vast majority of officers join up as officers.

Officers, as much as possible, have to be representative of the civil establishment. It is important that senior officers can deal with politicians and establishment figures on an equal basis. Even the captain of a mercenary band must be able to negotiate with prospective employers.

Unfortunately the attributes that are well thought of by the civil establishment are not always those that define potentially good officers. In most armies, particularly those that have recently had a violent change of government, party loyalty has provided a better route to promotion than have the usual military virtues. The greatest example of this was that of the International Brigades of volunteers for service in the Spanish Civil War. These generally high-minded and courageous soldiers deserved better officers that those they had, most of whom were selected for their loyalty to the Communist Party.

The British army throughout most of its history has been officered by wealthy aristocrats, such people who would hardly want to rock the political boat. The result has been a tradition of loyalty to the state, but this boon has been at the expense of the occasional high-ranking idiot.

An army's ORs can come into its ranks either as volunteers or as conscripts. Volunteers will enlist for a longer period than conscripts, in fact in the British army some will serve twenty-two years. Some, on the other hand, will only serve for a specific campaign, being basically mercenaries. The problem with voluntary enlistment is that the army has to compete for recruits with civilian employers. This has resulted in the British Army usually being under strength. In years gone by poverty swept many men into its ranks. This is no longer the case, at least not in Britain or the rest of the western world, and there is now a tendency to fill vacancies with immigrants and foreigners. This is a tendency that must be closely watched.

From the army's point of view the problems with conscripts are the opposite from those with volunteers. There is no shortage of conscripts, but they can be very unwilling. The great disadvantage is that they only serve a short time, usually one to two years. So they spend most of their time training, the best soldiers are fully occupied training them, so despite their large numbers there are few of them available for duty. Most significantly there is a growing world-wide repugnance for the concept of enforced military duty, but many states will retain conscription for the non-military purposes previously mentioned.

Conscript armies can cause problems in that they can reflect public opinion too much, and if public opinion has become highly enraged against an enemy then that war can tend towards primary warfare, but if, to prevent this, the soldiers are kept too much in hand then they may lose interest in the war.

Reflecting public opinion, as conscript armies do, makes it dangerous for governments to use them against popular discontent.

A further problem with conscription is that it disrupts the nation's economy.

All the above refers to what may be termed the 'field army'. Armed forces can exist on several levels below this. Most commonly will be militarised police, usually called Gendarmes. They can be regarded as second rate soldiers in terms of horizontal war, and good soldiers in terms of vertical war.

There may also be a militia or civil guard. This may be set up by a totalitarian regime as a mechanism to control the population, or, by a non-totalitarian regime, as a way to allow the settled population to defend itself against raids by guerrillas, either from within the country or from across the border. An excellent example of this type was the Kikuyu Guard which defended very well against Mau-Mau terrorists.

Further, this kind of militia can be a source of recruits for the field army and can carry out some personnel selection and initial training.

Another type of military organisation would be a cadre tasked to stay behind and organise a resistance movement in the case of the country being overrun by invaders. Such a cadre was set up in Great Britain in 1940 when an invasion was expected.

There may be many variants to these themes, some of which will be mentioned in subsequent chapters, but the most significant factor is always the field army.

Once a soldier has been discharged either from the regular or conscript service he will be placed on the reserve. The idea is that in the case of a national emergency the reservists will be called back to their units. This worked very well for the British army at the start of both world wars, in fact the BEF that went to France in 1914 contained 60% reservists, and the BEF was noted for its efficiency. But in both 1914 and 1939 the army had full public support. In 1956 this was not the case. 20,000 reservists were recalled for the Suez crisis and there was a large number of refusals. Worse, a large percentage of those that did report for duty were very unhappy and this had the effect of making the action even less popular with the public. However problems with the reserve did not alter the government's policy.

The USSR has always relied heavily on massive numbers of reservists. They have been called out three times since 1945: in 1968 for the invasion of Czechoslovakia, in 1979 for the invasion of Afghanistan, and in 1980 for the projected invasion of Poland. None of these occasions can be regarded as a success.

The first, the most efficient from a military point of view, occurred at harvest time. Russian farming is very labour intensive and the call-up was followed by a disaster for the food supply.

The second resulted in many Muslim reservists from the southern states of the USSR being sent to Afghanistan where their sympathy for their co-religionists hampered operations and made the war unpopular at home.

The third was an administrative foul-up and seems to have resulted in the proposed invasion of Poland being abandoned. The facts of the government system not working, people escaping obeying orders and the stirrings of democracy in Poland not being stamped out, will have played a part in the break up of the USSR.

From these examples it can be seen that a military system based on reserves can never be quite as reliable as one based on a standing army. Reserves, however, are very cheap, and will always appeal to planners. Some countries, such as Switzerland and Israel, make such a system work. In these cases the armed forces have the full backing of the population, and the reserves train a few days each year.

An army based on reserves, with their penchant for democracy and their low level of training, is almost a reversion to a militia showing a militia's weakness. The result will be a blurring of the people/army divide.

Governments usually have little choice as to the nature of

their armies, but in so far as they have they will have to balance military efficiency against any potential threat to civil order. Broadly a militia, as long as there is a degree of democracy, is no threat to the government but will be weak militarily. A regular army is good militarily but in countries with weak and unstable governments its officers may frequently aspire to coups. In this context the British system, a regular army officered by aristocratic amateurs, has been very successful.

It is something of a paradox that though, from the outside, armies may seem to be grey masses of conformity, from the inside they take great pains to build up the individuality of each soldier to ensure that he plays his part in the functioning of the military machine. Appendix 1 tries to illustrate the internal workings of the British army from a human point of view. It is a common complaint of ex-servicemen that they are nobodies in civil life and many find it difficult to adjust. This was most notable after November 1918 when there were large numbers of foot-loose ex-soldiers not being adsorbed into civil employment. These men were available for the *Freikorps*, in Germany, the Palestine Police, in Britain, and a host of other para-military organisations. Since the Great War mass demobilisations have been handled more carefully. A large number of ex-servicemen can be a welcome stabilising factor in a state, but they can easily become embittered.

The existence of a large number of military pensioners is of no military significance in modern western countries, but it has been important during colonial wars and may still be so in potentially unstable countries. Pensioners tend to be loyal to the government that they have served and still pays their pension. This fact was as useful to the French in Algeria as it was to the British during the Indian Mutiny. A revolutionary government must make cast iron guarantees to these men before their loyalty will change. Conversely any government that finds itself in a potentially revolutionary situation would do well to take steps to reassure its pensioners.

There are options outside the conventional ones of volunteers and conscripts troops. They will be tried only under exceptional circumstances. They are mercenaries and allies.

The word 'mercenary' when applied to soldiers carries various overtones. For the purpose of this study these soldiers will be taken as men serving in foreign armies, on short term contracts, and attracted primarily by the pay. Mercenary soldiers currently find extensive employment opportunities in Africa, and there are various companies, mostly operating in South Africa and having rather bland names, that specialise in putting together such units. At the time of writing there is something of a boom in this sort of employment in Iraq, and a private navy has been set up to defend against Somali pirates. Mercenary troops are not currently important in European context, but if the trend for armed interventions around the globe continues they could come into their own.

It may be that globalisation will encourage the growth of mercenary forces. It is apposite to recall that the British Indian army, which during the Second World War became the largest volunteer army the world has seen, had its origin nearly two centuries earlier as a few security guards for the Honourable East India Company's warehouses.

The advantages of employing mercenaries are that they do not have to be paid during peacetime, and their casualties are not a political liability. The disadvantage is that they are unreliable and so should only form a small part of any country's army.

The other unconventional option is allies. To ask an ally to shoulder a deal of fighting that a country's troops cannot handle may seem quite sensible and is commonly done. It usually starts with individual advisers, and steadily increases until large fighting units are deployed. This can be fraught with difficulties for the future as the ally will usually have his own war aims and sooner or later demand satisfaction.

It is, then, not surprising that most countries prefer if at all possible to raise their own forces by the usual options of either volunteer enlistment or conscription. Further, despite all other considerations, any government indulging in mass or protracted warfare must impose conscription sooner or later. This was true of all the major belligerents in the World Wars except India. It was, for example, true for the USA in the Vietnamese War; even Australia had to apply a selective draft to maintain its small force in Vietnam. The decision to impose conscription is a difficult political one, but if taken during peace time it is a definite statement that the government is prepared to fight.

3

What is a War?

A war is a period of intelligently directed sustained military operations undertaken on the orders of a government in pursuit of a political aim. A war will only be ordered by a government if it has been following a particular policy, understanding that that policy may cause conflict that would ultimately lead to fighting. Such a policy may be called an exercise in Power Politics. Initially there will be at least two sides in a war. There will be the aggressor, who has decided that his war aims are worth fighting for, and the defending side which is reacting against the aggressor.

A war, then, requires two governments that are prepared to fight to achieve their war aims.

It can be seen that, once the victor's war aim has been achieved then, logically speaking, the war has finished. Of course the real world is not that perfect and war aims sometimes evolve during the fighting, the Great War being a good case. The converse can also be true in that if a truce is declared while the differences between the combatants have not been resolved then the truce is apt to be only temporary. It can sometimes be difficult to determine the difference between one long war and a series of short ones. The Hundred Years War and the Arab-Israeli wars could well be describes as either. These considerations are made much more complex when alliances are involved.

Further, series of wars can be looked at from different angles which throw different lights on their nature and continuity. The Napoleonic wars illustrate this. They can be seen as an extension of the Revolutionary wars, one long fight against the *'ancien regime'*; as wars of aggrandizement, expressions of French nationalism; or as a long duel between England and France with Napoleon defending for France the fruits of revolution that England wanted to destroy. Finally they can be seen as a vehicle for the personal ambitions of Napoleon and his family. The extent to which they may be regarded as one long war will alter with which model is adopted. A remarkably similar set of models can be assembled to describe the Second Word War. However the importance of such considerations is debatable.

While the usual image of a war is one of a clash of uniformed troops, wars can involve the employment of part-time irregulars indistinguishable from civilians except when they are actually fighting. The important factor is that the war is directed by a government in pursuit of a political aim. So, whereas the Viet Minh guerrillas fighting the French in Indochina were fighting a war, the Baader-Meinhof gang, murdering people in Germany, was not.

It has been observed in an earlier chapter that there are two fundamental types of wars, they spring from the two fundamental types of inter-governmental relationships. They will be considered here in greater detail.

Horizontal Wars.

These are usually international wars, being wars between governments on the same level, usually national governments, or alliances. In such wars the task of the armies is usually to conquer and occupy territory. In total war this would involve the destruction of the enemy's army, but this is not necessarily so in limited warfare.

Vertical Wars.

These may be termed insurrectionary or internal wars though neither term is really appropriate. They are usually fought by a sub-national government trying either to replace the national government or secede from it, as has recently been seen in Yugoslavia. During the first twenty or so years following the Second World War, while there were still colonial empires, the bulk of these wars were indigenous people fighting against their colonial governments. This period has now passed but these wars seem to show no sign of fading away.

In order to be able to fight a horizontal war it is necessary for a nation to have some sort of hierarchical social structure. The war will justify the social structure and improve social cohesion,   yet it is possible that the social structure will be the cause of vertical warfare if the people start to resent it.

There are cases of wars that show the characteristics of both types. A civil war, such as the Spanish War, may start as a vertical war as the insurgents conquer some territory, but the war becomes a horizontal one between the government's area and the insurgent's area. Conversely in the case of an asymmetric war, a country might be invaded via horizontal warfare, but will continue resistance against the invaders via vertical warfare. However the principle of achieving the war aim remains the same.

In the case of a civil war one government fights to retain, or extend, its control over the whole country, the other either has similar aims or prefers secession. Secession occurs usually when one part of the country decides to be self-governing and breaks links with the central government.

Both horizontal and vertical wars have certain characteristics. Most obviously they result in a great increase in state spending and consequent increase in the power of the government. If the war is successful the political spread of government will increase as all sectors of society will rally behind it. It can happen that a government which is experiencing a degree of vertical conflict, that is whose people are showing signs of dissatisfaction with it, will go to war primarily for the purpose of rallying support. However if the war is unsuccessful then, as happened with the Argentinian experience of the Falklands campaign, disaster for the government may follow.

History illustrates this point by showing that states that fight few national wars often have many civil wars, revolutions and other civil upheavals, for example Spain and some South American countries. History also shows that democracies do not have wars with other democracies, probably because it is hard to demonise an open society. But despite this, since the end of the Second World War democracies have shown themselves more likely to resort to arms in a crisis than authoritarian states were. Probably the greatest reason for this is that authoritarian states can suppress discontent whereas democracies must divert it.

The attitude of a belligerent government to vertical warfare in an enemy's camp is at first sight surprising. While it may encourage resistance movements in territories the enemy has conquered it will often show little enthusiasm for similar action in the enemy's country, and may actually discourage it when the enemy's country is invaded even if regime change was the purpose of the invasion. The reason for such behaviour is plain when it is realised that the primary concern of any government is power, and a successful resistance movement could well produce a rival government. The Soviet Union would not even aid resistance movements based on communist parties. Such movements could be worryingly democratic and had to be carefully kept away from the Soviet population.

The Soviets carried this line of thinking to an extreme in the treatment of their partisans. The Germans overran vast areas of the USSR and large numbers of Russians became partisans harrying them. When these areas were reconquered by the Red Army most of these partisans were incorporated into the army as special assault units, and they suffered very heavy casualties. Those that were too old or unfit for military service were disarmed and scattered.

More recently, during the Vietnamese war, even though North Vietnam consistently encouraged the insurrection in the South, when they invaded the Viet Cong were elbowed to one side and excluded from government.

Refusing to help resistance movements can reasonably be held to have lengthened the Second World War by many months and caused very many casualties. This is just one example of how politicians will accept any number of military casualties rather than endure any kind of political setback or embarrassment.

Aiding a resistance movement can be very effective, as the Americans demonstrated by aiding the Afghan resistance against the Russian occupation. Unfortunately this instance shows that the long term effect can be unpredictable.

Another remarkable aspect of most types of warfare is the general reluctance of belligerents to attempt to assassinate the head of the opposing government. Of course it is not that easily done. It has been written that Saddam Hussein survived over a hundred attempts on his life and this gives an idea of the difficulties involved. Even so it must be concluded that governments prefer not to make war directly against other governments in order to maintain the spirit of reciprocity and the spirit of international diplomacy.

In vertical warfare, particularly in a *coup d'état*, assassinations are more likely, and most likely in a terrorist campaign, which is to say the kind of campaign least like war. However it must be noted that the attempt made by the Provisional IRA to assassinate the British Cabinet in 1984 did not win any support on the international stage, and this was detrimental to them as they desperately needed foreign sympathy and support.

Roughly similar comments may be made about bribery. It has died out as a serious consideration in horizontal warfare, but may still be important in some aspects of vertical warfare.

In secondary warfare in general, and in horizontal warfare in particular the relationship between war and politics, and the army and the government, is as laid down by the Prussian general Karl von Clausewitz in the early part of the nineteenth century in his book '*Vom Kriege*'. Essentially the army does what it is told by the government in order to forward state policy. The deployment of troops and the start of fighting only come after normal political pressure has been found to be ineffective. War, to quote Clausewitz, is '*a continuation of political discourse*', and political intercourse is the expression of state policy. Consequently it follows that the strategic direction of the war is totally subordinate to state policy. Quoting Clausewitz again, '*policy is the guiding intelligence and war only the instrument*'. This would be reassuring if all politicians and soldiers always behaved rationally, but unfortunately they don't. Even worse, public opinion, which often drives politicians, can be almost irrational. Further it means that as the war aims become more total, as with the Unconditional Surrender policy adopted by the Allies during the Second World War, so military methods become more like those of primary warfare, as with the bomber offensive.

Unfortunately Clausewitz died before finishing his book, so his ideas might not have been fully developed. He was extensively quoted, but it may be suspected not much read, in the years prior to 1914, and this led to two misconceptions.

Firstly, it became generally accepted that warfare was a reasonable way of adjusting international relationships and, being just another step in the political process, it attracted no more moral stigma than the writing of a diplomatic note.

Secondly, one of his chapter headings stated the '*War is Merely the Continuation of Policy by Other Means*'. Possibly if Clausewitz had lived longer he might have changed this wording. This statement gave senior officers the intellectual justification to take the view that war actually moved out of the political sphere and followed its own logic. This misconception will be considered later.

These concepts were welcome in countries like Great Britain where due to the rise of the middle class the upper class was starting to look redundant. It was welcome because the upper class was the officer class and the legitimacy of war justified the position of the officer in society. The upper class, on the basis of general prestige and newspaper ownership, was the opinion forming class, consequently the concept of war it accepted was accepted by the country as a whole.

Clausewitz and his writings are very well known and, accepting his narrow view of warfare as being national and rational, define well the relationship between warfare and politics. However from a modern perspective his work has two great limitations. One being that he hardly mentions guerrilla and revolutionary warfare. Remarkably his account of Napoleon's retreat from Moscow hardly mentions the Cossacks despite the undeniable importance of their perpetual harassing attacks. These omissions reflect the fact that at that period of history, except in thinly populated and underdeveloped areas, irregular warfare was not a real problem. This, of course, would change.

The second limitation is that he lived before the information revolution so he is not aware of the importance of the manipulation of public opinion, and the consequent reaction to any involvement with the war shown by the mass of the people.

The intensity of a war commonly varies with the emotional involvement of the people. There is a significant difference between horizontal and vertical warfare in that in the latter case the insurgent government will usually do its best to generate a real degree of hatred among its people and armed forces against the government it is fighting, as is illustrated by Appendix 2. This may well have a bad effect on post-war society. For horizontal war, as much as possible governments prefer the rational, unemotional approach. Small wars in far-away places carried on with professional troops will be restrained affairs and the government will be able to make rational decisions about them. However, if a government sees an advantage in it, it may well escalate the war, particularly if it is losing. To make this escalation acceptable to the people it will increase its propaganda effort. If this is not done carefully the propaganda, and the expectations raised by it, may push the government further into escalation than it really wanted to go. The German invasion of Poland in 1939 is an example of this, and will be considered in the next chapter.

Such considerations as these show how a spirit approaching to chivalry, at least among senior officers, can grow during a horizontal war. Conversely a vertical war, in which everyone's position in society may be subject to dramatic change, can be expected to only breed hatred.

As wars become larger so the war aims must become more emotional and sweeping, and hence more simplistic. Huge armies of conscripts will not endure long casualty lists, and the people will not accept the travails of warfare on the basis of a negotiated adjustment to the balance of power or some similar compromise. Rather, as the Second World War showed, they must be fighting for something like the Unconditional Surrender of what they are told is totally evil. Unfortunately such propaganda only strengthens the resolve of the other side, and the level of intensity of fighting will increase.

It is this public involvement, and enthusiasm, which makes the costs, both human and financial, of a war so wildly out of proportion with war aims. Very few governments will ever have the courage and control to disappoint its people but rather will revel in their new popularity until the war is definitely won (Falklands), or the people show signs of disenchantment (Vietnam).

It is not easy to predict how any society will react to

casualties in its armed forces. For example Victorian Britain was genuinely shocked by the casualties of the Tirah campaign (1897-1898), the Sudan campaign ('96-'98) and the Boer War ('99-'02), each casualty list longer than the previous one. But the country endured the much greater sacrifices of the Great War with scarcely a whimper.

Warfare at an extreme degree of intensity is termed Total War, and this may be regarded as the civilised version of primary warfare. In theory every member of the nation would be contributing in his or her way as much as possible to the war effort. That this ideal situation is never achieved is illustrated by numbers of wartime industrial disputes or cases of sabotage, theft or hoarding, but the government will certainly aim to achieve it.

A successful war will usually greatly enhance the standing of the government and confirm the existing social system. In fact some governments have gone to war primarily for these reasons. This may not be obvious at the time. George Orwell, who was a percipient social commentator, believed that Britain's participation in the Second World War would evoke a socialist revolution, and he was certainly not alone in this. When this didn't happen he expected the government to become 'fascist'. That didn't happen either, it is countries losing wars that are apt to suffer upheavals.

This trend towards primary, or total, warfare was shown in Great Britain and the other major combatants during the Great War. The British army, which before the war had been a small regular force, was dramatically expanded, initially by voluntary enlistment, later by conscription. Conscription required the legal system to become a part of a very coercive state, as did the mobilisation of labour and state control of industry. Unfortunately this very process of gearing up for modern warfare rendered the government almost helpless in the face of the huge people/army machine it had created, and this was shown by Prime Minister Lloyd George's fumbling and ineffective efforts to control Field Marshal Haig and the army in France.

The development of industrial war during the Great War also had the effect of making factories and the workers in them appear legitimate targets. The most essential aspect of secondary warfare is that armed forces fight each other and civilians are left out of it, but now armed forces could reasonably be used to massacre the opponent's civilians. This concept was pursued ruthlessly in the Second World War in the bombing of German and Japanese cities, and was aided and abetted by an increasingly bitter public opinion.

It would be a comfort to note that this doleful trend towards primary warfare was caused by the setting up totalitarian states harnessing the energy and emotions of their populations, and in the case of conventional warfare this may be true. However if nuclear warfare is taken to be the ultimate manifestation of primary warfare then it must be agreed that there is no need for a psychologically prepared and highly organised population, just a small technological elite, a determined government and one finger on the button.

The final contribution of technology to warfare is still in doubt.

As the end of a war approaches so the intensity of the fighting sharply declines. No-one wants to be the last to die, and a 'live and let live' situation prevails. It may be that at Appomattox some of General Lee's soldiers loudly proclaimed that they would fight the Yankees till hell froze over, but they were a small minority. It is also true that there have been the occasional *Gotterdamnerung* scenes such as the final Soviet assault of Berlin in 1945, but in general once the outcome of the war is no longer in doubt then the fighting fades away. This is largely because the soldiers on the losing side will fade away, if at all possible. If not then, in the case of a national war they will stop fighting and surrender. In the case of an internal war they will swap sides.

The difficulties of the post-war settlement will be considered later.

An example will now be given to illustrate some of the points made in this and the previous two chapters.

The Chechen Wars

Chechnya has existed under several different names, but for the sake of simplicity this is the only one that will be used in this study. It is a small state of population around 1,100,000, mostly Sunni Muslims.

Chechnya was annexed by Russia in the 1870s and has had a stormy relationship with Moscow ever since. After the break up of the USSR in 1991 Chechnya's status was vague, and in September of that year militants led by the former Soviet General Dzhokhar Dudayev stormed the government building, killed a leading communist, drove out the rest of the government, and installed a nationalist government. Next month Dudayev became president.

While Chechnya was a Soviet Republic it was actually fused with Ingushetia. This joined the Russian Federation, and Chechnya declared full independence in 1993.

Chechnya faced several problems. Probably the greatest in the long term was that the population was not homogeneous but contained a large minority, of ethnic Russians and other non-Chechens, of about 23% of the population. A shorter term problem was that Chechnya was in a strategically important location, being between the Caspian and Black seas, and between Russia and the oilfields of Kazakstan and Azerbaijan. So Moscow would want to keep Chechnya in line. Finally and immediately Ingushetia was having a border dispute with the Russian Republic of North Ossetia, which threatened to involve Chechnya.

Soon after 1991 ethnic violence between Chechens and the

ethnic minorities broke out and almost developed into actual warfare. President Yeltsin tried to send in some Russian troops but Chechen forces would not let them leave the airfield. Finally Dudayev expelled all Russian troops from Chechnya. Unfortunately they left behind several large armaments depots. Despite the increasing lawlessness Dudayev announced a general amnesty for all criminals. This made Chechnya a magnet for a variety of desperate men. The upshot was something approaching the ethnic cleansing of the non-muslim population. There were attempts at pro-Russian coups in 1992 and 1993 but they were crushed by force. Industrial production went into steep decline as many Russian and other non-Chechen engineers and other industrial workers left. The Russians had large numbers of troops close by due to the border disputes of the neighbouring states, and they started to assist the opposition factions who, in 1994, mounted two assaults on the capital Grozny. Both assaults were defeated, but fighting had reached such intensity that the Russian president, Boris Yeltsin, decided to send in Russian troops to 'restore order' (the classic excuse) in December 1994.

Interestingly there was widespread criticism of the decision, some senior officers even resigned and hundreds of junior officers and other ranks were discharged for refusing orders.

The Russian troops were totally unprepared for this invasion, and were badly briefed as to what to expect. From the first the invasion did not go well even though the Chechen air force, such as it was, was destroyed on the ground. The Chechens were very well supplied with anti-tank weapons and, as many had served in the Soviet army, they were well trained in their use. Russian armoured columns were subjected to many ambushes in the forests and hills *en route* to Grozny. The Russians reacted with excessive use of firepower. They killed lots of people and hardened opinion against them.

They finally surrounded Grozny and the climax of the

campaign was to be its assault. This commenced on 1st January 1995. The city was attacked by four widely spaced armoured columns. The theory being that the shock of fast moving armour would deter resistance. It was a disaster. Three of the columns were halted in the narrow streets by anti-tank teams hitting the first and last vehicles then stalking the rest that were now trapped. The Russian infantrymen seem to have been reluctant to leave their APCs, and when they did they had little idea of how to go about urban warfare.

The fourth column reached the centre of the city unopposed. Then it halted. The Chechens closed in and placed it in something like a state of siege. 20 of its 26 tanks and 102 of its APCs were destroyed. Only around 100 of its original 1,000 soldiers escaped. The day's fighting caused at least 2,000 Russian casualties, some estimates are as high as 5,000. It also killed a large but unknown number of civilians, mostly ethnic Russians whom the Chechens were using as human shields. One of the casualties was the Russian column commander who was killed by a mortar shell.

The Russians pulled back, considered their experiences and reorganised into battalion-sized infantry assault units. Then three days later they attacked again. The battle continued until 7th March 1995 and left the Russians in charge of a bomb site. They admitted to losing 1,376 dead, including a major-general. The fighting cost the lives of around 35,000 civilians.

After Grozny the war spread to the southern, more mountainous, areas of Chechnya, and began to bog down. A change in character came over the Chechen forces resisting the Russians. They became more Islamic, and an anti-Russian Jihad was declared. Muslim volunteers started to enter Chechnya to fight for it.

The almost indiscriminate violence of the Russian troops caused unease among the other Russian Republics, and a series of terrorist spectaculars brought the problem home to the Russians. Unfortunately for the Chechens this terrorist activity had an unintended effect in that several nearby republics that had been sympathetic to their fight, now regarded them with suspicion and barred their entry.

The war progressed for over a year and the Russians occupied around two-thirds of Chechnya. But by May 1996, considering world and Russian opinion, and the expense of the campaign, President Yeltsin was looking for a way out. As the Russians showed signs of becoming conciliatory the Chechens staged two coups. On two occasions they infiltrated roughly 2,000 fighters into Grozny, placing the Russian garrison under siege. On the second occasion the Russian relief column suffered heavy casualties. President Yeltsin signed the ceasefire agreement a few days later. The truth was that Chechnya had achieved independence.

Peace may have been declared, but the internal power structure of Chechnya had changed. Now the most powerful men were two of what are commonly called 'Warlords', and they controlled the Islamic militia which had formed during the war. In August 1999 they invaded the neighbouring Republic of Dagestan in support of Islamic separatists.

This invasion was a failure in the face of Dagestani militiamen and Russian firepower, and the invaders returned to Chechnya. The Russians followed them, and in October 1999 the Second Chechen War started.

There can be little doubt that the new Russian President, Vladimir Putin, benefited from this decision for war. Recent events had been humiliating for the Russians, and the people wanted to see a demonstration of Russian power, as well as an action to hit back for a number of terrorist atrocities which were all blamed on Chechens.

The initial Russian plan was restricted to overrunning the flat, northern, part of Chechnya. This the Russian armoured forces did quite easily, but if the campaign had halted there it would have been pointless, so the Russians had to advance to capture Grozny. They did this carefully, wanting to avoid the heavy casualties of the first war. Each step was preceded by an artillery barrage. They occupied villages and towns round Grozny, cutting it off from the outside world. Then they systematically reduced it. By February 2000 it was in Russian hands.

From then on the final stage was crushing the guerrillas in the mountains, and it is a matter for speculation as to what extent this has been achieved. Both sides had their weaknesses. The Russian public was wearying of the war, and the government of the cost. The Chechen resistance, being partly nationalist and partly Islamic Militant, was increasingly prone to internecine feuds as Chechen society in general became more clannish in nature.

Regardless of the on-going insurgency a pro-Russian government was installed and Chechnya became a part of the Russian Federation. Peace and Victory were declared.

The three wars are estimated to have caused 20,000 military deaths. Estimates of civilian deaths run as high as 100,000. It also caused hundreds of thousands of people to flee their homes, lose everything they had, and endure great hardships. The minorities were reduced from 23% to less than 6% of the population. The situation at the end of the war was much the same as it was at the start, except that the Chechen population, being more homogeneous and less law abiding, was now a more formidable potential enemy.

The Chechen wars are of interest in that they bring out points made in chapters 1 to 3 about social structures, armies and wars.

On the map Chechnya looks like a conventional nation, but as soon as the unifying force of Communism was stripped away Nationalism began to be replaced by Militant Islam.

This Militant Islam was developing into an extra-national force which would cause plenty of trouble for the Russians. The Russians could have handled Chechen nationalism more easily, but the casualties they had caused among the nationalists in the first war were at least partly the cause of its decline *vis-a-vis* Militant Islam.

The Chechen troops were mostly either reservists or militiamen. There was little difference between them. Their stand in Grozny in the first war, and their effectiveness as guerrillas, were impressive. The Dagestan war showed their limitations in a conventional offensive.

The Russian troops were, initially, conscripts. This went a long way to cause the unpopularity of the first war. For the second they had been largely replaced by volunteers and mercenaries. Not only were they better soldiers and suffered fewer casualties, but they made less of an impact on public opinion.

Finally the three wars considered here can be seen to have been really one continuous one, but one whose nature steadily changed as the driving force of the Chechen government changed. This driving force evolved from Communism to Nationalism to Militant Islam, changes which should have been anticipated and planned for by the Russians. Whether this war, or series of wars, really has come to an end or is just having a truce will depend largely on the policies of the Russian Federation and the degree to which it can conciliate Chechen nationalism and Islamic militancy.

4

Why Fight (War Aims)?

Wars do not just happen, rather they occur because a government decides that it has certain aims and ambitions that it is prepared to wage war to achieve, that the cost of the fighting will be small enough to make it worthwhile, and that the population will support, or at least will not actively oppose, the war. The question of public support is not so important in the case of totalitarian states where the people do as they are told, but it is in a democracy where the government will have to invest a lot of time and effort explaining its actions.

Also there must be a victim state that will fight back.

These aims and ambitions that governments fight for are termed 'War Aims', and their attainment, or otherwise, is the measure of success of the war. Although when precipitating a war the aggressor government will balance its cost against potential advantages, it is unlikely that any government will start a horizontal (national) war unless it expects a quick and easy victory. The situation with vertical wars is rather more complex. The war aims may reflect sensible government policy, but may reflect the government caving in to a hysterical pressure group or to public opinion in general. The difficulty in telling these apart will be obvious to anyone enquiring into the origin of the American Civil War.

There may be several war aims and they will usually exist at two levels. These may be called the Public and Real war aims. The Public war aim must be simple and include an obvious appeal to justice and/or patriotism. The Real war aim will be just that, an aim followed by government policy over a long period of time. It will be judged necessary by the government but would not be expected to engage national enthusiasm. The concept of Public and Real war aims, and their difference, will be illustrated below by a consideration

45

of the British decision for war in 1914.

When the Public and Real war aims coincide then the nation will be showing a unanimity which will make it an efficient war machine. This coinciding of war aims can occur when a country has been invaded, and explains to some extent how right can sometimes put up a good fight against might, as the Finns did so convincingly against the Soviets in 1939-1940.

When a protagonist has several war aims they will stand at different points along the Public/Real scale. This is handy for the government during the war as it enables it to pick out the appropriate one to justify its actions. But after the war it can result in a degree of confusion and even disenchantment.

There are two circumstances that complicate war aims. The first is protraction of the war. As the balance of power between the belligerents, and the level of escalation, change so war aims can vary. At least the Public aims can vary, the Real ones are much less likely to. Secondly are complications brought about by alliances. Each protagonist will constantly review his war aims with a view to improving his post-war bargaining position. This will make a common policy difficult. For example in the Second World War the policy of Unconditional Surrender was not a particularly logical one, and it seems that it was only adopted because Roosevelt 'railroaded' Churchill into it at Casablanca during a press conference, Churchill not being able to think fast enough, or not having the strength of purpose, to reject it. Later, Field Marshall Montgomery was to call this policy a 'tragic mistake'.

In addition to these two circumstances must be considered Stupidity, one of Karl Marx's driving forces of history. This is surprisingly frequently shown by politicians when their rhetoric has backed them into a corner to get out of which they must either fight or endure a degree of humiliation. Many politicians have sent soldiers out to die rather than endure even a little humiliation.

For horizontal wars, war aims fall, very broadly, into five categories:

To occupy territory for its own sake.
To entirely change the nature of the victim government.
To extend political influence in the surrounding area.
To consolidate and legitimise the government's position, usually by civil war.
To improve the government's standing with the people by undertaking a popular action and exploit the tendency for the people and government to unite against a common enemy.

These categories are not mutually exclusive and should be clarified by a few examples.

The Iraqi attacks on Iran (1980) and Kuwait (1990) were simple attempts at property theft, driven by oil, and it is almost certain that the future will see similar actions driven by oil. Another cause of war will be water, increasingly so as the world's population increases. An example of this was given by the digging of the Jonglei canal which became one of the causes of the Sudanese Civil War in 1983.

After the Second World War both Germany and Japan were occupied for several years while their systems of government were restructured. Simple regime change is a less dramatic version of this. The invasion of Iraq in 2003 was the result of a decision that Saddam Hussein's government had to be replaced. The Iraqi wars will be considered again before the end of this chapter.

In 1978 the USSR deployed a largely Cuban-manned armoured task force in Ethiopia for the Ogaden war. The USSR was not remotely interested in Ethiopia *per se*, but was hoping that it would be a base for the spreading of communism throughout Africa.

The American Civil War (1861-1865) was a standard civil

war. It was caused by several states deciding to leave the Union because of legislation concerning slavery, and the remaining states not accepting this secession.

The Argentine invasion of the Falklands in 1982 was undertaken to boost the popularity of the military government.

These five categories of war aims can only cover the immediate aims, and cannot explain the deeper motivation to war. This point is illustrated by the Iraqi invasion of Kuwait in 1990. They would not have attacked if the Kuwaitis had not suddenly started to flood the market with oil, in disregard of OPEC treaties, thus reducing the price of oil and threatening Iraq with bankruptcy. The Kuwaitis seem to have taken this action as a result of the Iraqis not repaying their massive loan required for the Iraq-Iran war.

The general complexity of war aims is well illustrated by the actions and motives of Great Britain and the Central Powers, Germany and Austro-Hungary, in 1914.

As is well known the march to world war was started by the assassination of the heir to the Austrian throne. However, before that the government of Austria-Hungary had decided that the very existence of Serbia, in that it might act as a magnet for Pan-Slavism, was a threat to the survival of the Austro-Hungarian empire. The Austrians were heavily involved in the area having annexed Bosnia in 1908, consequently the assassination was used as a pretext to occupy Serbia. This occupation was to be the method by which political pressure could be brought to bear to destroy Serbia as a viable nation. This would stabilise Austro-Hungary by reducing the extent of Pan-Slavic agitation. Unfortunately Russia was an ally of Serbia, and the Russians made it plain that they would support Serbia in the case of a war. The Russians had their own agenda and planned to expand southwards essentially to expel the Turks from Europe and annexe Constantinople. They actually started their mobilisation several days before the declaration of war.

Austro-Hungary could only think of attacking Serbia because it had the backing of Germany. But though the Germans stood to gain by the emasculation of Serbia, Pan-Slavism was not their problem, the Russian Steamroller was. In the decade before 1914 industrial progress in Russia had surged ahead and Germany was becoming worried that she would lose her position as the leading industrial power in Europe. The Germans knew that, sooner or later, they would have to fight to prevent Russian expansionism. The German stance was basically defensive, but if possible they would hope to conquer some Russian territory, the requirement for *lebensraum* was already a feature of German policy, and set up Polish and Baltic states independent of Russia but presumably dependent on Germany, to set Russia back and advance Germany. Germany just wanted to retain her position and regarded war as an essentially defensive measure, that is a 'Preventive War'. The Germans knew that as their potential enemies were growing stronger by the day, so if they were going to act, it had to be soon. It can be noted that Bismarck believed that a preventive war was like committing suicide through fear of death!

The major strategic problem for the Germans was that France was Russia's ally and, still smarting from 1871, was looking forward to a war to recover Alsace and Lorraine. So fighting Russia inevitably meant fighting France. To handle this problem the Germans planned to inflict such a disaster on the French army that France would be quiescent until the armistice was signed. Initially, again, the Germans stance was defensive so that the French would attack and be defeated. Unfortunately the military logic demanded striking the French left flank so the Germans marched troops through Belgium. They knew that this would be viewed with concern by the British Government.

There is little doubt that the Germans dreaded a war with Britain, but they took a gamble. They hoped that Britain would stay out of the war. If not they hoped that the war would be over before Britain had time to expand her army and her munitions production to continental standards. It could be that they overestimated the importance of the Curragh Incident of March 1914, when over fifty officers tendered their resignations when told that they might be called on to coerce Ulster into Home Rule, and believed that the British army was in disarray. If so they were wrong.

Both Germany and Austro-Hungary were trying to solve by war problems that had built up in peacetime. The situation for Great Britain was strikingly similar though the background was a little more complex.

In 1914 Great Britain and the Empire were in a parlous financial condition. The essential logic of empire, with Britain the manufacturing country and the colonies providing the raw materials, was starting to fall apart. The problem was that capital was more profitably invested in the colonies or other developing countries than in Britain so there was little available to update manufacturing plant. Consequently, in terms of industrial manufacture, Germany had overtaken Britain.

Two results of German industrialisation were the huge growth of their merchant fleet, a challenge to British supremacy, and the growing importance of the Mark. The two great props of the British Empire, control of the seas and of banking, were starting to look a little shaky. In fact, due to the dramatic spread of railways, trade could flourish throughout Europe and Russia totally independently of sea-routes and the Bank of England. But worse was to come. By the early years of the new century the importance of oil had become obvious. In fact the Royal Navy was in the process of changing from coal to oil, and the world's first oil-driven battleship, the Queen Elizabeth, was launched at Portsmouth in 1913. The Empire, huge as it was, did not include any large oil fields, but the Middle East, most notably Iraq (Mesopotamia) did. The Germans knew this and initiated the *'Drang nach Osten'*.

The German eastern impulse took the main form of the Berlin-Baghdad railway, and this was regarded as a major threat by HM Government to the security of the supply of oil which it regarded as very much in the British sphere of influence. Iraq at the time was still a part of the Ottoman Empire, which provided a good reason to dismember that empire. The Berlin-Baghdad railway, being a railway, was immune to any threat from the Royal Navy, Britain's primary strength. It was also the reason for the German hostility to Serbia which was an obstacle to its construction.

The German alliance with Turkey, a necessary part of the *Drang nach Osten*, was enough to send shivers down the spine of the Foreign Office. It raised that spectre of a huge Islamic army threatening Egypt and India. Both countries were of great importance to the Empire, and both were prone to civil unrest which would hinder defence.

All in all senior politicians, bankers and business men were coming to the conclusion that it was intolerable that Germany should become more powerful and she had to be stopped, if necessary by a war.

In 1914 throughout the span of living memory living conditions for both working and middle classes had steadily improved, consequently the general prestige of the government, regardless of party, was high and few would question its decisions. However it is undeniable that the years before 1914, in particular 1912, had seen some very bitter strikes and labour disputes. In one case 300,000 workers were locked out of cotton mills in Lancashire, and in another a miners' strike resulted in over a million workers being laid off. In view of this there can be little doubt that many in political circles found the unifying effect of a war very welcome.

British public opinion was largely anti-German. This was the age of universal literacy and cheap newspapers, so caricatures of foreigners would be easily believed, particularly so as the mass of people was not yet in a position to travel overseas to see through these caricatures. Tension was created and maintained by a succession of story books about German invasions of Britain and other such fantasies. This tension enhanced by a series of blunders, like the Agadir crisis, precipitated by the Kaiser's government, and the development of the *Kriegsmarine* which was seen as a direct challenge to the Royal Navy. The Conservative Party, more imperial than the government in its outlook, shared these feelings and was very suspicious of German ambitions. It is ironic that this opinion was formed when the Germans were actually worried about losing their position in Europe.

The British government was Liberal, not in general in favour of a war, but it had only a small majority in the Commons. When it became apparent that there would be a European war, the cabinet, and the parliamentary party, were divided about what action to take. It is true that Great Britain and other powers had guaranteed Belgium's neutrality in the Treaty of London in 1839, but the British Foreign Office view, expressed shortly before the war, was that the treaty did not oblige Britain to defend Belgian neutrality 'in any circumstance and at whatever risk.' For a while the Germans, quite reasonably, regarded this treaty as *'un chiffon de papier.'* Certainly German war aims did not provide a sensible cause, but there was a reasonable fear that if Germany could defeat France and become pre-eminent in Europe then she could make life difficult for Britain. The Conservative opposition, with public opinion behind it, spoke with one voice demanding war. The government was shaken by several resignations, and fearing defeat in the Commons used the invasion of Belgium as a pretext for war, and sent a small, by continental standards, expeditionary force of one cavalry and four infantry divisions to France. As soon as Britain was in the war the German war aims changed in such a way as to justify, at least at the time, Britain's part in the war. Britain exercised far more diplomatic leverage while staying out of the war, and if she had continued to do so the war might have been much less destructive.

Great Britain declared war on Germany as a result of the latter's invasion of Belgium in August 1914. The war the British government declared was a rather modest affair, but it very quickly escalated into something approaching total war. By its ill-considered decision, based more on party political expediency than a sound appreciation of the situation, the government set in train an irreversible tragedy. Of course once the war had started no politician wanted to propose a compromise to stop it as doing that would be admitting that the deaths, suffering and cost were unnecessary. So the war became self-perpetuating.

British sensitivity about oil is illustrated by the fact that within 48 hours of the declaration of war with Turkey, which occurred on 5th November 1914, a brigade was landed at the estuary of the Shatt el-Arab, and it quickly occupied the local Iraqi and Persian oilfields. Further, as soon as possible, in April 1915, British and Empire troops launched the Gallipoli campaign in an attempt to knock Turkey out of the war. If this had succeeded it would have blocked the *Drang nach Osten*, removed any Islamic threat to the Empire, enabled the western allies to send supplies to Russia and keep that vast country in the war, and secured Iraqi and Persian oil. Britain could then reasonably feel that she had achieved her war aims and could look for a negotiated end to the war.

It was important to keep the Russians in the war against Germany. There was always the fear that her huge armies could be otherwise employed. In a worst case scenario they could march against Iraq, Iran, and finally against British India. Unfortunately the Gallipoli campaign failed and the war had to be fought out to the bitter end on the western front.

In 1914 governments thought in terms of the Clausewitzian dictum that war was just an '*extension of political intercourse'*, and that declaring war was a reasonable way of adjusting the relationship of the nations. The morality of war seems not to have been considered. The question is how much has changed since.

The British decision for war in 1914 illustrated the difference between Public and Real war aims. The Public war aims included the principle of self-determination for small nations and making the world safe for democracy. The Real one was the destruction, or downgrading, of a commercial rival. As John Maynard Keynes, the famous economist, wrote in 1920, *'there is nothing very new to learn about this war or the end it was fought for; England had destroyed, as in each preceding century, a trade rival.'* It is true that when men are asked to enlist and risk death they will need a Cause, not a few points on the balance of payments deficit, but the logic of the fighting will follow the real war aim. This explains how so often the cost of a war is wildly out of proportion with the advantage to be gained from the stated war aims.

The folly of divergent Real and Public war aims was shown after the war when the British army was involved in restricting the right of self-determination for Ireland and India. The first resulted in the Blacks and Tans, the second in the Amritsar Massacre. These could not be hidden and played their part in creating the feeling of disillusion about the war.

A favourable public opinion may be regarded as necessary for the initiation of a war, at least in a democracy, and it is usually generated and manipulated by the government. However there are occasions when the public has been more militant than the government and this has ensured that the government had to fight, like it or not. For example there is no doubt that the British government had to initiate a campaign to liberate the Falklands after the Argentine invasion or be voted out at the first opportunity.

This was similar to the situation of the British government in

1939. The Second World War can be said to have been the indirect result of the peace settlement following the Great War. Large areas of Germany had been taken off her and incorporated into other countries. Most significant among these were the Sudetenland and the corridor which should have linked East Prussia to the rest of Germany. The German population as a whole did not relish the idea of another war, but there can be no doubt that every German was unhappy with this situation and when the National Socialists came to power they set about rectifying it. Their initial policy was to expand the borders of Germany to include all the ethnic Germans living close by. The critical point came with the Munich Pact of 1938 which resulted in the German reoccupation of the Sudetenland. This was widely held by the British public to have been a betrayal of Czechoslovakia, however if it had resulted in 'Peace in our Time' it would have been soon forgotten. Unfortunately it was followed by the invasion and occupation of the rest of that country. This was justifiable to the Germans as Czechoslovakia was starting to fall apart with neighbouring countries staking territorial claims which would have resulted in potentially unfriendly countries occupying land almost within Germany. This invasion was regarded, in Great Britain, as a gross breach of faith by the Germans and in particular by Adolf Hitler. It generated a wave of public anger and, in the face of this the government, anxious not to appear complacent, guaranteed Poland's borders against invasion.

This invasion was almost inevitable. The Germans wanted a corridor through to East Prussia, and although the British Government had urged the Poles to grant this they refused and decided not to yield an inch of Polish territory. In view of the state of their army this was rash. Unfortunately, by his extreme propaganda, the Fuhrer had manoeuvred himself into a position he did not want to back down from, and the result was that, in 1st September 1939, the Germans invaded. Great Britain issued an ultimatum demanding that the Germans evacuate Poland immediately. They didn't, so the British government, itself not being able to back down because of public opinion, declared war on Germany, on 3rd September 1939, dragging France in as well. This was despite the fact that neither Great Britain nor France could take any practical measures in support of Poland. Well might Hitler, on being informed of the declaration of war, look stunned and ask *'Was nun*?'

Embarrassingly, a fortnight later, on 17th September 1939, the Russians invaded Poland. Rather inconsistently war was not declared on them.

Once again the logic of the fighting followed the real war aim which was the same as in the Great War, to downgrade Germany as a commercial rival. At the end of the war Poland was occupied by the Red Army, and the Russians were even less welcome there than were the Germans. If the war had really been about Poland then Great Britain would have to admit to losing it.

Although it would be difficult to maintain that the invasion of Poland merited unleashing the Second World War, there can be no doubt that war would have come sooner or later because of the Fuhrer's belief in the necessity of acquiring *Lebensraum*. His view was that Germany was over-industrialised, too many people were employed in manufacture, consequently Germany was dependent upon exports. Further, he believed in the thesis of Shrinking Markets. This was the belief that as third world countries acquired the means of manufacture they would be less dependent on imports so the exporting countries would be chasing fewer customers. Therefore if Germany were dependent on exports it must, sooner or later, being a commercial rival, come into conflict with Great Britain, then the USA. The way round this was to become self-sufficient, or at least as self-sufficient as possible, and this was to be done by seizing *lebensraum* to the east, particularly in the Ukraine.

The large rural areas of *lebensraum* were to be populated by ex-soldiers and farmers, the original Russian population would be side-lined. The vastly extended countryside would complement the industrialisation of the German cities by providing food, raw materials including oil, and markets. Further, these markets would not shrink, because the Germans would not allow industrialisation in the *lebensraum*, and what industry there was, left behind by the Soviets, would be destroyed. Acquiring *lebensraum* would render exports largely unnecessary and so remove this cause of possible conflict with Great Britain, a conflict that Hitler particularly dreaded. But unfortunately the first step towards *lebensraum* had to be through Poland. The first step towards a policy which was to make unnecessary a war with Great Britain was the very act that caused one.

Whatever interpretation is placed its start, the war steadily expanded and was ultimately responsible for 54,800,000 deaths (Guinness Book of Records), though it might be argued if the 7,800,000 Chinese deaths should not be included, their war being independent of the World War. The essential point is that the war would not have happened if a small group of men had managed diplomacy a little more sensibly.

International wars, even those involving complex alliances, can seem simple compared to some civil wars that can hinge on the definition of the states fighting them.

For example the Korean war (1950-1953) was caused by there being two Korean governments resulting from the *de facto* partition of Korea following the Second World War. Both governments wanted to demonstrate that they were the legitimate government of the whole country. South Korea was effectively restrained by the USA, but, as the communist situation became favourable the North Korean government was encouraged, by China, to press its claim, initially by a guerrilla campaign then by invasion.

Usually the war aims are simpler. In 1960 Katanga seceded

from the Congo. The Congolese government decided not to allow this and, after three years of confusion and fighting, Katanga returned to the fold.

In any situation involving civil strife a government's first consideration is the security of its own position. Consequently civil wars often tend to be more brutal than necessary. When the warring sides subscribe to different political systems, things become even worse. Following the French debacle of 1871, the voters of Paris, dominated by the working classes who, having no work to do during the Prussian siege of the city, and all being armed and enrolled in the National Guard, elected a left wing local government, the Commune.

Observing this the French government moved out of Paris to Versailles and started to assemble a loyal army. The time-lag granted to the government by Communard inactivity was essential as the troops on hand made it plain that they would not fight against the Commune, and one general who ordered them to was captured by a mob and finally shot.

Objectively it could be seen that the Commune could not last long in the middle of a deeply conservative, even monarchist, country like France in 1871, but the government wanted to teach the Communards a lesson. When the troops assaulted Paris, between 20,000 and 25,000 Parisians were killed in the first few weeks, and many more were executed or exiled over the next five years. After this France was stable and could start planning for the next war with Germany.

In civil wars fighting can break out almost spontaneously as if by mutual consent, but not so with international wars. As the events of 1939 illustrated, once the aggressor government has rationalised its war aims it will set the pace by making a series of demands, creating tension and political conflicts, so that it becomes clear that that government believes that it has a *casus belli*. With the benefit of hindsight it is remarkable that so often the actual invasion comes as a complete surprise.

In the face of political aggression the defending government has two main courses of action, appeasement and deterrence. Appeasement, despite the opprobrium usually heaped on the concept, is actually the normal way of handling international tension. Basically the defending government ascertains the cause of the aggressor complaint and considers what it can do to defuse the situation. This can, of course, be carried too far, as it is usually believed the British and French governments carried it too far before the Second World War, but the principle is not necessarily bad.

No matter how much the aggressor is appeased some deterrence will also be required, and generally it is remarkable how little. Deterrence consists of making it plain that if a government is attacked it will fight back. The victim state may plan to fight back in a purely military way, as was done in the Falklands, or by mobilising an international alliance against the aggressor, as in the Gulf in 1991, but the intention must be made plain. In these two cases deterrence failed. In the first the Argentinians took the view that the British no longer had either the means or the commitment to retake the islands. In the second case the Iraqis believed that the world would look on with indifference. In both cases the attackers were mistaken, if the defenders had made sure that there were no grounds for misunderstanding then the invasions would not have taken place.

If the defending side observes that its diplomatic options are failing it might decide that it is necessary to make a pre-emptive attack. This can make it difficult to determine who is the aggressor, particularly as many acts of naked aggression are styled as pre-emptive attacks.

Once the initial assault has taken place the options for the defenders are simplified. To fight or not to fight. The Czechs, quite reasonably, did not fight in 1967 when the Russians invaded. Unfortunately occupations by foreign troops are not always that blatant particularly as there will usually be a part of the population which will welcome them.

The Germans achieved the invasion of Austria, the *Anschluss* of 1938, without violence because many Austrians believed that joining the two countries was sensible. The Germans then bloodlessly invaded the Sudetenland to 'restore order' when that disorder had been caused by the German minority acting under orders. The fast deployment of troops following a propaganda offensive was the Fuhrer's speciality. In both these cases the population accepted the new *status quo*.

More recently, in 1962, the Egyptian army invaded the Yemen in support of a *coup d'état*. The invasion seemed to go smoothly but, if some welcomed the Egyptians, others fought against them and, after heavy fighting and many casualties, they left in 1967. The Soviet experience in Afghanistan was similar. They arrived in 1979 and left in 1989.

A major problem for the defending government is how the people react to an invasion. If the government does not fight, or only fights half-heartedly, then it could be that the people, mounting their own resistance, will ultimately be more of a threat to the government than the invaders were. When the Japanese invaded first Manchuria in 1931, then China in 1935, the Chinese Communist forces were in very poor condition. They grew in strength fighting the national war against the invaders. It is quite possible that without the Japanese war Mao Tse-tung and the Chinese Communists would by now have been long forgotten.

All the above has been written in terms of a war between nations, but it applies just as well to vertical warfare. In such a case war has in effect been declared when an organisation has been set up which is able and prepared to launch a violent anti-government campaign. Governments, in the final analysis, govern on the 'divide and rule' principle, and can usually emasculate such organisations by political manoeuvres backed by force and appeasement. However if a united front of all malcontents can be set up then 'divide and rule' no longer works. After that it comes down to a trial of strength.

As a general rule the vulnerability of a state to vertical warfare varies with its degree of development. As a state becomes more highly developed there will be more state employees, pensioners and people on benefits. These people are natural loyalists, so as their numbers increase so the state becomes more stable. Few modern western countries are vulnerable to vertical warfare. However the development of the state machinery can go too far until everything is run by a huge state bureaucracy and the people are ground down in poverty. When this is the situation there will be seething discontent which may result in an uprising. In broad terms this is what happened in the USSR between 1989 and 1991. Unfortunately for a repressive government this is apt to occur when it is trying to liberalise, loosening the chains which gives the malcontents their chance.

In the modern world where even financially poor governments can deploy extensive firepower it is almost impossible for a guerrilla movement to succeed without foreign assistance. This gives an international dimension to wars which might seem at first sight to be purely domestic affairs. This was the context of the American involvement in South Vietnam, and this is worth some consideration.

After the French defeat and withdrawal from Indo-China in 1954, South Vietnam was set up as an independent non-communist nation. Whether it stayed like this was not that important when seen from a world perspective at the time. This changed when some communist leaders, in China and other countries, started to talk about the setting up of a large and bellicose Communist Bloc including China, Indo-China, Burma, Indonesia and other south-east Asian countries.

Indonesia withdrew from this as a result of a confrontation with the British over Malaysia.

It was a widely held view in the late 1950s that if South Vietnam fell to the communists several other countries would follow, like dominoes, and the feared Bloc would come into existence. The US support for the South Vietnamese government was the means to the quite reasonable end of preventing this. Also it may be that they welcomed the chance to restore their military prestige following the 'Bay of Pigs' fiasco.

The Americans can be criticised on two counts. Firstly the South Vietnamese government was corrupt and incompetent and the Americans should have forced it to improve. Secondly it may be suspected that they took the bombast of the Communist leaders too seriously. In democratic countries, where the Freedom of the Press obtains, politicians must talk reasonably sensibly. Communist politicians are not inhibited like this, and this might have led the Americans to think that they could not weaken or break up this planned Bloc by diplomatic or economic measures. Whether or not these criticisms are justified the result was a tragedy.

The American involvement in Vietnam illustrates the unfortunate effect of creeping escalation of commitment (mission creep). They started sending a small number of advisers to South Vietnam soon after 1954, and this number was steadily increased because it was easier to do this than to alter the policy which would have been, to some extent, admitting defeat. The motivation of North Vietnam is usually taken to be that of a *guerre sacrée* based on nationalism or communism, but it should be noted that North Vietnam could hardly feed its own population and really needed the paddy fields of the south.

The international aspect of vertical warfare is further complicated an extra-national organisation ensconced in one country takes military action against another, and the injured party retaliates. This type of action will be considered at greater length under the heading of Asymmetric Warfare in a later chapter.

Regardless of whether the war is of the vertical or horizontal type there will usually be some sort of incident to spark off the actual fighting. This incident might be highly contrived, or it might be what would otherwise be an inconsequential accident. In 1969 the final score in a football match touched off a war between Honduras and El Salvador. The war was not about football but a whole raft of tensions mostly based on migration of Salvadoran people looking for work in Honduras. It was short but even so several thousand people, mostly civilians, died. After it both countries dramatically increased their defence budgets.

Conversely pretext may be dispensed with and an invasion come as a complete surprise as when North Korea invaded the South. But this will only happen if the aggressor government does not have to worry about public opinion.

Once the fighting has started both governments will have to publish their war aims if they have not already done so. The more cynical and controversial they are, the later they will be published. This is to take advantage of the way that fighting tends to rally public support behind the government.

A clear statement of war aims is necessary for the sake of public opinion and for negotiations with allies and neutral countries. In a long war these war aims might change which causes governments a good deal of trouble. The achievement, or otherwise, of war aims provides a measure of the success of the war.

A short sharp war is always aimed at, but if a war drags on the government will worry that the people might get weary of it. Its usual reaction is to tell wilder and wilder lies about the other side, which, of course, will reciprocate making negotiations that much harder to start.

The language of propaganda can form an interesting study. For example, in an attempt to downgrade horror, the expression 'body bag' has, in the US, morphed into 'human remains pouch', then to 'transfer tube'! As Salvador de Madariaga said, *"no-one has ever succeeded in keeping nations at war except by lies"*.

So far in this chapter a number of examples has been given to illustrate various aspects of decisions for war. They do not, though, show these in terms of the possible results of historic continuity, and this will be attempted with a brief summary of the recent history of Iraq and Iran.

The Allies invaded Iran during the Second World War to ensure oil supplies and maintain an important route for transporting war material to Russia. The Pro-German Shah was removed and his son, who was only 22, was set up in his stead. After the war the Anglo-Iranian Oil Company, which became BP, received very generous concessions from the Shah. Seeing this, and failing to secure better terms, the elected Iranian government which followed the Shah's, nationalised the Anglo-Iranian Oil Company's assets. This was difficult for the British government of the time to complain about, it was Labour and was itself at the time involved in a vast program of nationalisation. However this new Iranian government was soon replaced and the succeeding one organised, with the help of the CIA, a coup that set the Shah's government back in power. The AIOC and now the US enjoyed even better oil trading terms.

Unfortunately though the Shah's government did enact some reforms that looked good to westerners, such as improving the lot of women, it was secular, pro-American and pro-Israel and this evoked a great deal of opposition, particularly as Islam was becoming more militant. Ultimately this opposition, under the leadership of Ayatollah Khomeini, staged an uprising which swept the Shah from power.

Following the fall of the Shah the US was humiliated by the holding for over a year of 52 American hostages, mostly embassy staff, and the failure of a daring helicopter special forces rescue mission. Consequently, when the Iraqis under Saddam Hussein went to war with the Iranians, they were supported and supplied by the US.

The Iranians had had their revenge on the US, now the US was taking its revenge on Iran.

The Iraqis then invaded Kuwait in 1990. The position of the USA was initially one of indifference. The US Ambassadress, April Glaspie, passed a broad hint to Saddam Hussein a few days before the invasion that the US would take no action. The US warned the Kuwaiti royal family of the impending invasion so that they had time to escape with their valuables. However the Kuwaiti government was not told, and when the invasion did occur it turned out to be against the wishes of the US. Perhaps all this was the result of incompetent diplomacy, but the position of the US was that the client had now turned against his benefactors so Saddam Hussein had to go. The 1991 campaign was a model of its kind and the troops halted at the borders of Iraq as it was confidently believed that Saddam and his government would fall. This did not happen, so a round of trade sanctions was imposed and this, predictably, rallied the Iraqis behind the Saddam government. Consequently the next campaign was launched in 2003. Justifying this campaign was not easy. At first it was to be a part of the 'War against Terror', even though Saddam had steered well clear of Al Qaeda. Then the pretext was 'Weapons of Mass Destruction that could reach London in 45 minutes'. These weapons turned out to be non-existent. So it was then simple regime change. Regardless of pretext the US would have its revenge. Saddam Hussein ended his life on the gallows, and the whole area entered a period of general instability.

With Iraq occupied by the US and British forces, Iran started to provide active aid to insurgents in Iraq to make life as difficult as possible for the invaders. Following this invasion, it is not surprising that Iran, which was designated by President Bush II as part of the 'Axis of Evil', is determined to become a nuclear power.

It is remarkable that the three key decisions, the Iranian decision to humiliate the US, the US decision to back Iraq and the decision to depose Saddam Hussein, were not taken on the basis of the existing situation but rather on the basis of recent history. It is quite reasonable to believe that the governments involved should have been able to take a more penetrating view, even if this meant managing, and to some extent, disappointing, public feelings.

5

Sub-Conventional Warfare

Before considering the main theme of this and the next chapter it will be useful to recapitulate what has been written in earlier chapters about the nature of secondary warfare. The basic definition of Secondary War is intelligently directed sustained military operations. Such a war will be initiated when a government believes that achieving its war aims is all but certain and will more than compensate for all the deaths, suffering and other losses caused by the war; and the victim government resists. It is an essential thesis of this study that secondary warfare forms only the violent extreme of the full range of inter-governmental conflict. The bulk of this range does not even consist of what would usually be considered as fighting.

This range of conflict consists of any actions taken or ordered by one government to alter the behaviour of another government or society. It is obvious that to produce what would be recognised as a real war there must be two governments capable of very hostile behaviour. If the coercive behaviour is very one-sided and the victim government rolls over and accepts the new situation, there may not be a war, but there will certainly be some resentment even if right at the non-violent end of the scale. When the Russian troops invaded Czechoslovakia in 1967 there was no conventional war, but there was still a simmering conflict which ensured that the situation remained unstable.

This definition of secondary warfare as a part of the full spectrum of inter-governmental conflict means that it can only be understood in terms of that spectrum, and the range of that spectrum can include all methods available and all the variety that human ingenuity can think up. This conflict is aimed ultimately at the opposing government but in the shorter term it can be aimed at any or all of the government, people or armed forces. Different methods are used against each target. Diplomatic notes, speeches at the UN, the formation of alliances and such methods act against governments. Propaganda, trade embargoes and terrorism can work against the people which will then bring pressure on the government to change its ways. A campaign of bribery and corruption and low grade harassment can degrade the efficiency of the troops, particularly if dissension can be sown between the ranks. This can be most effective if senior and junior ranks are of different race. As its faith in its armed forces decreases so the government will become more malleable.

The aggressor's political campaign will start with low key political measures, speeches, protests, petitions and the like. It may involve rearmament and an arms race. It will proceed through terrorism, assassinations and guerrilla warfare. It may include trade sanctions and economic warfare, and psychological warfare, then long range actions like bombing and finally up to conventional warfare. In theory the last stage would be Nuclear Warfare, and moving out of the secondary warfare spectrum.

It is often said that arms races cause wars. This is no more true than saying that declarations of war cause wars. Arms races are aspects of a government's policy, not the cause of that policy.

The critical factor is escalation. A government will escalate the conflict if it has the means to achieve its aim and can carry the people with it. Clearly a highly developed government which is able to coerce its people can be more aggressive, but internal conditions and relationships mean that this is seldom obvious at the time.

Conversely it can happen that public opinion, fired up by government propaganda, is actually more belligerent than the government which might then feel pressured into continuing the war, or even escalating it, when it would have been more sensible to initiate negotiations. This may well describe the situation in Great Britain between the German invasion of Poland and Pearl Harbour.

The Second World War began on 3rd September 1939 when the British declared war on Germany. Throughout the next 27 months, during which the British acknowledged that they could not significantly attack Germany, the Germans made several rather ham-fisted attempts to negotiate a peace. There is every indication that they would have been offering a surprisingly reasonably settlement, but Great Britain ignored them. There is no doubt that every individual British man and woman felt that he or she had to 'stick it' to finally put an end to the German wars, a determination enhanced by the new and wide use of radios which broadcast news, propaganda and speeches, and gave the population a real feeling of personal involvement. Also throughout the bulk of this period the government was led by an aristocrat who had every reason to want to destroy a country that seemed to be making socialism work. The fact that it was easy to see that the sacrifices involved in waging war far outweighed any possible gain, seems to have been ignored.

Both horizontal and vertical warfare may pass through all the stages listed above, but with horizontal warfare, which is usually national war, it is a major step up to actually start fighting a conventional war. It is true that few conflicts are preceded by a formal declaration of war, but even so the size of the step up is always obvious. Because of this a government planning conventional aggression always goes to great lengths to ensure that the public is on its side, and it will ensure that there is an incident, no matter how contrived, that will make it look as if it has been forced into the action.

Even though it is true that both forms of warfare can pass through these phases there is a clear tendency for horizontal (national) wars to involve conventional warfare. Vertical wars will be more likely to involve guerrilla warfare and other forms of war of lower than conventional intensity. These forms of warfare are lumped together under the heading of 'Sub-conventional warfare' and are the subjects of this chapter. Conventional warfare will be considered in the next.

Warfare in general is complex but sub-conventional warfare gives the impression of being even more so. It can occur in both the horizontal and vertical contexts. The less important of the two is the horizontal context and this will be covered first.

Such warfare will occur across the borders of neighbouring countries that are involved in some kind of conflict. It will involve small units, regular soldiers or irregulars, fighting small scale actions, cross-border raids and ambushes, conducted over wide areas of the less civilised parts of the world. The governments involved will usually be of the less well established kind, or what are termed 'warlords'. Such fighting is widespread, not very important, and little reported. The most important case that affected Great Britain was the Confrontation with Indonesia over the establishment of Malaysia.

The Indonesian aim was, by making raids across the border into Borneo, to destabilise that state and, ultimately, annex it. Borneo was defended by British and other Commonwealth troops. Some fighting did occur in other parts of Malaysia, but most took in Borneo and involved vicious but brief actions in thick jungle. It lasted from 1962 to 1966, and cost the defending forces 91 lives, 19 of them British, and the Indonesians approximately 590. Civilian casualties were remarkably low, being put at 36 dead, which reflects the small number of civilians living in the jungle. Carrying on the Confrontation was very expensive and brought about the collapse of public finances in Indonesia, and with that the collapse of public order. The Indonesian president, Sukarno, too collapsed while making a public speech and the large communist party, believing him dead, staged a *coup*. The *coup* failed. For it to succeed the insurgents needed to kill eight leading anti-communist generals, they only managed six. The army fought back, and around half a million people, mostly communists died. This resulted in a new Indonesian government which ended the Confrontation.

Another common application of sub-conventional warfare is as an auxiliary to the conventional forces of horizontal warfare, in the way that Wingate's Chindits were. Naturally in this context it is fairly arbitrary when sub-conventional operations come to be regarded as conventional; it will depend on the size of the units involved.

However it is in the context of vertical warfare that sub-conventional warfare is most important. This mode is vastly varied but it usually boils down to an insurgent government trying to replace the current one. There are variations but this is the most common case, and the classic scenario for vertical warfare. Perhaps the most common variation would be a spontaneous resistance movement against a foreign invader, but this will have to conform to the insurgent government model or ultimately fade away.

It is common to describe such a war as a revolution, but this is a misuse of the word. A revolution is a basic change to the structure of society which occurs in a short period of time. This change may well require armed force to carry it through, but the state terrorism involved falls outside the warfare being covered here. A revolutionary government usually achieves power by force of arms, this is almost necessary because if it came to power by constitutional methods there would have been little need for a revolution. It is this process of achieving power, replacing the incumbent government, which is the war, not the revolution that may follow.

Insurgent governments can be broken down very roughly into two types, which may be labelled 'Nationalist' and 'Revolutionary'. The nationalists are usually fighting against a foreign colonial-type government and their aim is solely to get rid of it, and not change society otherwise. The

71

revolutionaries want to reorder society and getting rid of the government is the first step to doing this. As a rule the revolutionaries will provide the extremists and will set the pace of military action. The nationalists will be the more likely to be classified as moderates. The moderates will have carried out the early agitation and constitutional struggles and may well look askance at the younger extremists, who will look on them with irritation. Insurgents of these two types may combine to remove the government, but may very well fight among themselves afterwards. This was the basis of the Irish Civil War that followed the Anglo-Irish War.

In usual cases of vertical warfare there is only a small number of fighting insurgents, but these are aided and abetted by a large number of supporters. For the insurgency to be successful there must be a steady progress of supporters willing to become active fighters. It is the purpose of the security forces to stop this flow. Military action will try to kill the active fighters at such a rate that few people will want to be one. Political action will try to make being one pointless. How this works out in practice is considered below.

Since 1945 the vast bulk of insurgencies has occurred in the context of the Cold War. That is, one of the communist powers, the USSR or China, has supported the insurgents, and the USA has supported the incumbent governments. In this way the super-powers could be conducting proxy war against each other. Since 1991 this kind of support has been less predictable.

There are two basic ways the insurgent government goes about its task. These two modes are not mutually exclusive and an insurgency will use either or both, or sway from one to the other as its circumstances dictate. These modes are Guerrilla Warfare and Urban Insurrection.

Guerrilla Warfare in the Countryside

To describe this case, in an attempt at simplification, a standard model is taken, the one usually called 'Communist Revolutionary Warfare'. This was shown at its most effective in the French Indo-China War, however it must be understood that its efficacy is easy to overrate. This brand of warfare runs through three phases: Political, Guerrilla and Conventional, although this categorisation of the phases might seem a little over-neat to those actually involved with them. Each phase will be considered separately below.

The Political Phase.

This is by far the most important of the three phases, in its early stages the greater part of activities involved will be legal and low-key, consequently the government will not realise what is happening. The aim of this stage is to create a revolutionary government even if this government is actually only governing a small percentage of the country's population. The process will start with a small but dedicated Communist Party and a generally discontented population. It is impossible to imagine this phase being any kind of success without some degree of general discontent. Initially the revolutionary armed forces are in the Aristocratic stage.

The revolutionaries will achieve the aim of the phase by setting up a united front, that is a political organisation consisting of all discontented parties, for example the Viet Minh. The Communist Party will then slowly, and quite possibly very violently, take this over. This will prevent any later extremist vs moderate tension. However, initially at least, it is important that the united front will seem to represent all classes and races involved in dissent.

Next will emerge a Strong Man, this is necessary to maintain unity and ensure that there are no factional schisms. Further it will ensure that there is an easily identifiable target for any aid that interested neighbours may wish to give. The people will be dragooned into accepting this new order. This is done by means of endless and simple, but highly effective propaganda, such as 'Land to the Peasants', by selective terrorism, and mostly by organising the people.

This phase may see an attempt at a *coup d'état*, or, if a good amount of popular support can be mobilised, a general uprising. However the chances of success are not great.

The great achievement of the political phase is the united front, but, in the long run this may contain the seeds of its own destruction in that it subordinates the interests of different races and other groups to the party. For example in the USSR the government initially seemed to be representative, in fact Stalin was a Georgian, but ultimately the USSR turned into an empire ruled by the Russians and fell apart.

An important tactical result will be the creating of an effective intelligence organisation. It is essential that the insurgents have sympathisers in government offices. In 1920 one of the IRA's supporters was a confidential typist for the Special Branch ('G' Division) in Dublin Castle, copies of important reports went direct to the IRA. But more important still than this is the building up of a picture of everything to do with the police and other security forces, their supporters and potential informers. Naturally communications must be set up to carry this information to those who could use it.

The Guerrilla Phase

A better expression might be 'The Armed Propaganda Phase'. The purpose of this phase is to convince a steadily increasing percentage of the population that they owe allegiance to the Revolutionary Government. That is they will pay taxes to the Revolutionary Government, carry out public works as ordered and provide recruits.

The guerrillas achieve this by removing the national

government's presence, by driving out or assassinating policemen and officials, and by attacking troops so that they operate in much larger groups and spend more time in their defended camps and AFVs, (Armoured Fighting Vehicles), so cease to influence the people. In attempts to discredit the government guerrillas will particularly target good officials, leaving bad ones in place, and will try to goad troops into repression and atrocities. Throughout this phase there will be no let up in the propaganda effort, which will be aimed at both sides.

This phase may demonstrate a degree of chaos that will make it difficult for the government to plan its campaign. There might be three separate types of guerrilla actions taking place simultaneously.

The guerrilla campaign against the government is the obvious one.

The guerrillas might be involved in fighting against political rivals in the way that the Communists under Tito destroyed the Chetniks, Royalist guerrillas, during the Yugoslavian fight against the occupying German army.

The guerrillas and their supporters might be running a campaign against anyone who could be seen as a supporter of the government. For example ex-servicemen living on a pension may be seen as potential informers. If such people are of a different race or religion to the guerrillas this could go so far as to see the minority massacred or driven out, fates suffered by many Protestants in Southern Ireland during the Anglo-Irish War and the subsequent civil war. This kind of low level strife can be very squalid and murderous, and can result in the polarisation of the population and even partition of the country. It will, though, result in the remaining population being solidly behind the guerrillas.

All these trends may be hidden by an increasing level of general lawlessness as people get access to firearms and the opportunity to settle old scores and do a little thieving.

Embarking on the guerrilla phase prematurely can be dangerous for the insurgency. Its armed forces will be in the militia stage and there in increasing numbers. If the political foundations of the insurgency have not been carefully laid the armed forces might slip out of control. This is broadly what happened in Ireland in 1920. The result can be schisms in the insurgency, ominous in the long term and making it vulnerable to the security forces in the short.

The Guerrilla Phase, if successful, should result in the setting up of a safe area, governed by the revolutionary government. It will be in an inaccessible part of the country, usually along the border with a state that supports and supplies the guerrillas. This state will also provide a safe haven which may be of critical importance, partly for R&R and partly as a base to launch raids from.

During the Soviet-Afghan War probably the major problem for the Soviets were large numbers of Afghans based in Pakistan and raiding into Afghanistan. The Soviets decided to break the link between these *mujahideen* and the rural Afghan population. They did this by depopulating rural areas by bombing, strafing people and livestock, and dropping large numbers of scatterable mines from aircraft. The countryside was also pummelled by artillery. As a result of this around seven million Afghans became refugees, and the *mujahideen* were deprived of some of their support. Doubtlessly this provided a short term advantage for the Soviets, but a good number of these refugees must have crossed into Pakistan and increased the *mujahideen* numbers.

However the guerrilla phase can tend to settle down to an equilibrium, the guerrillas controlling most of the countryside, and the government holding the towns. Such an equilibrium will inflict a significant rate of attrition on the government and, if that government is a colonial administration, that might be enough to force it to withdraw.

That is now a very uncommon situation. In general an equilibrium works against the guerrillas and this will force them to progress to the next phase as an alternative to slipping backwards.

The Conventional Phase

The importance of this phase is easy to exaggerate. In it some of the most proficient of the guerrilla forces are formed into conventional units and the government's army is directly challenged. It is impossible to launch this phase in any meaningful way without foreign support which is provided across a common border. This, though, may result in the foreign government expecting too much influence in the internal affairs of the revolutionaries who may ultimately feel pressured into accepting a compromise with the incumbent government rather than risk subjugation by their foreign ally.

Aid coming across the border may very well result in the government ordering raids into the adjoining country to prevent this. The great examples of this were the American-led raids into Laos and Cambodia during the later stages of the Vietnam War. Such raids do not have a lasting effect.

A common border with a friendly country is necessary for the Conventional Phase but it might seen that there was an exception to this rule shown by the entirely home grown IRA policy of setting up 'Flying Columns' during the Anglo-Irish War. However, despite looming large in Irish legend, the flying columns were little more than a waste of guerrilla resources. They will be considered later.

The Conventional Phase is useful for the revolutionary government to practice at being a real government and to gain credibility on the world stage, but the fact is that if these insurgent conventional units clash with government units of comparable size they will usually come off worst. The organisation and equipment that were hindrances to the government's troops in the guerrilla phase are now its strength.

This was much what happened in Yugoslavia in the Second World War. The partisan units became impressively large, but a hard fight with the Germans forced them to reverse the trend and go back to smaller units. This effect can occur in reverse. The poor performance of some Argentinian troops in the Falklands campaign has been blamed on their previous employment exclusively in internal security operations, that is in units too small for conventional warfare.

Of course it has happened that the insurgents' conventional troops have won, and the French Indo-China war was the great example. The battle of Dien Bien Phu was one of the greatest military triumphs of all time, but it was the last purely military triumph for Communist Revolutionary Warfare.

These three phases, political, guerrilla and conventional, are not discrete units that follow on one from after another but they will run at the same time, and, if unsuccessful the trend can be reversed, for example the conventional phase could be closed down and the emphasis returned to the guerrilla phase.

An example of how things can go wrong was provided by the Tet offensive of 1968. In this General Giap, commanding the North Vietnamese troops, decided that South Vietnam was ripe for a general uprising. So he organised one which came as a total surprise to the United States and South Vietnamese forces. The fact of this surprise, which was a considerable military achievement, shows how great the great public support for the communists was. Unfortunately there was no general uprising, the government troops fought back with great determination and the result was heavy casualties for the communists. The Viet Cong, the South Vietnamese Communist forces, suffered the most and it appears that this resulted in the North Vietnamese conventional troops having to take on a greater part of the subsequent fighting. After Tet there was certainly no reduction in the intensity of the fighting, but the communist forces could achieve no more than an equilibrium with the Americans, whose forte was conventional warfare. The eventual result of this was the withdrawal of both the North Vietnamese and US troops from South Vietnam under the terms of the 1973 treaty. In 1975 the North Vietnamese, pursuing their *guerre sacrée*, rather cynically carried out a conventional invasion of South Vietnam and conquered it, the Viet Cong not being in a position to maintain national independence. The South Vietnamese Communist government-in-exile, which was in Paris trying to conduct meaningful negotiations, was ignored, and the North Vietnamese Communist government now rules all Vietnam, and Vietnam, which should be a prosperous country, is one of the poorest nations in the world.

The example of the Vietnamese wars illustrates one aspect of communist rule in that the rulers tend to hold on to their positions for a long time. Vo Nguyen Giap was in command of the Vietnamese communist army from December 1944 when the first platoon was formed until 1972 when, apparently as a result of the failure of the North Vietnamese invasion of the south of that year, he was promoted to be Minister of Defence, a post with little real responsibility. He held that post till 1980. Such long tenure of office can result in the policy associated with that office becoming inflexible. In the current example Giap defeated doubters on his own side, the French, the US, and his colleague Van Tien Dung defeated the South Vietnamese in 1975. This singleness of purpose was impressive, but the cost to the people of North Vietnam of all these successes was very high, and some must find it hard to justify.

In the two cases where Communist Revolutionary Warfare has been successful, China and French Indo-China, the governments being fought against were weak, unpopular, repressive and deserved to fail. Unfortunately the governments that replaced them were even more repressive and tyrannical, but at least they were stable, in the short term.

It is difficult to know, particularly in the case of China, if there was an alternative. Could peaceful political action have brought about changes even if over a longer period of time. Perhaps not, but one thing is certain, the communists were determined to be in power, and the sacrifices of the people did not matter to them.

Communism itself, which demands unquestioning obedience and grey conformity from its minions, is not really a creed well suited to inciting a revolution, and as its nature has become more apparent since the 1950s this must go at least some way towards explaining its lack of success. Conversely communism is a very brutal creed and this fact has helped communist revolutionaries to maintain the draconian discipline necessary to sustain their cause. This is one reason why liberal/democratic movements, with their lack of discipline, seldom produce significant guerrilla organisations. That communism lacked any all-conquering magic was shown during the Greek Civil War. Militarily the insurgents were beaten when the neighbouring countries, particularly Yugoslavia, closed their borders, but there can be little doubt that when the Greek people saw the scale and quality of US aid they knew where their interests lay.

The result of Communist Revolutionary Warfare, a stable but repressive government was, naturally, illustrated by North Vietnam which brutally and very efficiently put down a peasant rising in 1956. The rising was in Nghe An, this was Ho Chi Minh's native province but that fact was of no assistance to the rebels who years of misrule had driven to desperation. Such governments may be held up as a yardstick for assessing the result of other regime changes brought about by sub-conventional warfare.

For example the Algerian Nationalists government has proven unstable and the country homicidally divided. The

Algerian War of Independence was fought with extreme brutality but even so the insurgents did not place the same emphasis on the political phase that communists would have done. The insurgent organisation, the FLN, was never really a mass movement and the Algerian Communist Party was small and unimportant. After independence came the emergence of militant Islam and more fighting. During the 1990s it is believed that 150,000 people died in the internal wars of this unhappy country.

The same lack of political preparation was shown in Cyprus. Here the governing power, Britain, was not really committed to fighting the insurgents and soon left. Thus there was not really enough time for the political phase, so it is not surprising that instability followed based on the Greek/Turkish racial divide. This conflict will be considered later, in terms of terrorism.

Cyprus was an example of what may be termed a 'War of Disengagement', a war fought by British and Empire troops during the course of closing down the Empire. It would not be an exaggeration to say that by the end of the Boer War it was appreciated that the Empire would not last for ever, but the social and commercial changes brought about by the Second World War, the great set-backs for European power and prestige, and promotion of native personnel, particularly in the army, meant that withdrawal from Empire was almost imminent, and that fact evoked the Wars of Disengagement.

Of these wars, Malaya was the biggest and Cyprus could be called the most squalid, but in all cases the aim of the British Government was to leave behind a friendly independent country and in this it was largely successful. There can be no doubt that in some cases the departure of the British was hastened by a guerrilla campaign, but there was never a military defeat. The insurgents created a 'situation', a challenge which the British government decided not to meet, but to pull back from. This was quite reasonable. The British Empire was based on trade and that would continue after independence. It is interesting to note that the great failure during the withdrawal from empire was in the one country where the issue was more land ownership than trade, Southern Rhodesia (Zimbabwe).

The problem of a racial divide mentioned above can be very important and will be considered later. Its relevance in the context of Communist Revolutionary War was illustrated by the Malayan Emergency, which ran from 1948 to 1960. Malaya contained a large minority of Chinese workers, and the insurgency progressed very well among them, but it made little progress among the Malay population. It may be that the communists did not try hard enough in this direction, but it is significant that the British Colonial government had to maintain its popularity by granting independence.

There was a sharp increase in Communist Revolutionary Warfare following 1945, mostly in the colonial empires, and this is usually put down to political causes, particularly, of course, by Communists. Actually it was mostly due to vast quantities of support and supplies from either the USSR or China given in a Cold War context. The fact is that major insurrections involving large numbers of full time soldiers and various other workers were not possible before the Second World War without this support. Most revolutionary areas were very poor and depended on subsistence farming. It was just not possible to feed a worthwhile number of non-productive people. In fact during colonial days, when an uprising seemed imminent the government had only to send a few troops to destroy some crops to bring the population to heel. The introduction of modern techniques, most importantly tinned food, made significant guerrilla warfare possible. It can be easy to ignore the fact that guerrillas need supplies in the same way that conventional troops do, though not in the same quantities. The communist guerrillas in Malaya were defeated by being cut off from their food supply, and it is difficult to imagine any insurgency moving to the conventional phase without sharing a border with a friendly state that was prepared to provide the necessary supplies.

In this context the collapse of communism in the USSR had a very beneficial effect in South and Central America. It resulted in Cuba no longer being able to subsidise various revolutionary movements the leaders of which then entered conventional politics, as for example in El Salvador.

Naturally it will be a standard security forces tactic to try to separate the insurgents from their supporters, but this will usually not be possible. It was achieved in Malaya by implementing an ID card scheme and concentrating the Chinese population in easily guarded 'New Villages'. Usually potential insurgent supporters are not so easily identified, and a similar scheme, 'Strategic Hamlets', run by the Americans in South Vietnam, failed mostly for this reason.

This policy of cutting guerrillas off from their supporters was the route to the British victory in the Boer war of 1899 to 1902. The fighting Boers were mostly farmers. Their families were rounded up and moved into camps, and their farm buildings and crops were destroyed. Initially this was only successful to a degree, at least the Boer guerrillas knew their families were being fed. Later when the farms had reverted to nature the families were returned to them and many Boers gave up the fight and returned home to work on the land to save their families from starving. Unfortunately this policy of concentrating the population caused a great deal of tragedy because the Boers, being used to living in the wide open spaces with little contact with other people, did not have the resistance to epidemics that urban populations develop. Consequently a large number of detainees died of diseases which should not have been lethal. This was believed at the time to have been a part of a British plot and has caused long standing bitterness.

During the late 1950s, following the communist victory in Cuba, some senior ex-guerrillas and party men decided that the Communist Revolutionary Warfare method could be dramatically changed to suit South American conditions. The Cuban campaign itself, though the revolutionaries were communists, was not an example of Communist Revolutionary Warfare, and certain protagonists, most famously 'Che' Guevara, thought that it would provide a model for further campaigns. Their idea was basically to put the Guerrilla phase before the Political one. The guerrilla band, that they termed a '*Foco*', would by its actions foment revolution among the people. The result of trying to apply this concept was failure, not least because other governments did not oblige by being as unpopular as was the pre-Castro Cuban one, or by having such poor armies. The guerrillas trying this method soon became little more than brigands, preying off the peasants that they should have been trying to recruit.

This is the common fate of guerrillas on the losing side. They become politically irrelevant. They are perpetually on the move and have to terrorise the locals just to survive. But this, naturally, turns the locals against them and hastens their demise. Such, for instance, was the end of the Mau-Mau in Kenya.

There is a variation on the '*foco*' concept, this being when the country is invaded by a small force containing the revolutionary leaders, the invaders not expecting to triumph by their own military power but by the discontented people rushing to arms in their support. As John Brown at Harper's Ferry and Dr Jameson in the Transvaal showed, this is a strategy unlikely to succeed.

There can be little doubt that, following the closing down of the colonial empires and the end of the Cold War, the limit has been reached for insurgencies based on the mass support of the rural population. Future insurgencies will be either '*foco*' or terror based, and in the unlikely event of one succeeding, the first task of the new government will be to convince the people that this was what they really wanted.

There is a further dimension to sub-conventional warfare, and that is urban warfare. Insurgencies based on city populations have had a very poor success rate. The real potential for the urban guerrilla is in preparing the way for an uprising, as will be considered in the next section, and not working up to conventional warfare. In the early stages, though, the difference will not be obvious.

The movements will start with a series of protest marches and politically based crime, like bank raids. This should result in government retaliation which will be seen as heavy handed and generate sympathy for the insurgents. But the next step can only be to set up 'liberated areas' like 'Free Derry' in Londonderry or Bab el Oued in Algiers. This is only possible if the security forces are either very weak or the government extremely conciliatory. However when the security forces are reinforced or the government takes a harder line then such liberated areas, despite insurgent *braggadocio*, are easily pinched out. This results in a dead end in town, and a withdrawal into the countryside.

The greatest difficulty with an urban insurgency is in the political phase. The leaders must show themselves. They must take a public part in organisation and decision making. So they will be arrested. The rest of the population, wanting a quiet life, will produce many tip-offs, as it is easy to do in a city. Urban Guerrillas can be effective in maintaining a resistance against an unpopular regime or, most effectively, against the forces of an occupying power, but not in revolutionary warfare.

The Urban Insurrection

The foregoing has shown how insurgent forces can be built up in the countryside so that they can ultimately challenge the government's forces. This is bound to be a lengthy process. It is much faster to challenge the government directly in its capital city. The government must stay in the capital otherwise it will cease to be the government, so the aim of the insurgency will be to replace the government there.

The simplest way to do this is a *coup d'état*. The members of the existing government are killed, induced to leave or thrown in prison, and their places taken by insurgent nominees. Then, providing the state organs will obey the orders of the new government, the job is done. A *coup* may fail for a variety of reasons, most commonly because some troops stay loyal to the government and defeat the conspirators. Also, commonly, due to poor security, conspirators might be arrested and the plot exposed. However on rare occasions the people in general can foil a *coup*. In 1920 occurred the Kapp *Putsch* ('*Putsch*' is the common word for a failed coup). During the post-war disturbances in Germany Wolfgang Kapp, a second rank politician, led a *Freikorps*-backed *coup* and drove the government from Berlin. The government quickly found that it would receive no support from the army which remained studiously neutral, so it called on the workers of Berlin to stage a general strike. This they did and it was highly effective, the city ground to a halt and Kapp could not even feed and pay his troops. After four days he left for Sweden and the troops marched away.

It is difficult to believe that the German army and civil service, both traditionally monarchist institutions, had no sympathy for the coup which was aimed against the republic. Unfortunately Kapp had made no practical preparations. He did not even have any typewriters or typists, let alone printers. The rubber stamps that German bureaucracy depended upon went missing when the clerks went on strike. Perhaps if Kapp could have made some sensible public pronouncements and held out for a few weeks then the army and other right wing elements might have rallied behind him. As an aside it might just be that, drawing the obvious conclusions from this, Adolf Hitler decided to set up the SS as a state within the state of Germany, an organisation that would continue to function despite a general strike.

A coup as purely a change of government would not seem to come within the purview of warfare, but in practice the *coup d'état* is only one extreme of a form of war often very brutal because of its personal nature. Further it is usual that the coup's supporters are military officers. When the army takes over the government there will follow a decrease in its efficiency in terms of its fitness for warfare as it can no longer separate military from civil considerations. This in itself may be enough to cause a war by inducing a greedy neighbour to provoke one.

The ideal case of an urban rising, and the opposite extreme from the *coup d'état*, would be a colossal riot so vast that the security forces would totally lose control of it, in fact soldiers sent to quell the riot would join the rioters, some may even hand over their weapons. The rioters would storm the governmental buildings, lynch its members, and replace them with some rioters selected by acclaim. There are two reasons why this scenario is very unlikely. The first is that the security forces will not be overwhelmed if only they, or some part of them, stay loyal to the government. Providing only that they defend essential buildings then, after a few days, the riot will blow itself out. Secondly there must be a government-in-waiting ready to step in and take over, and it must have the prestige to make its orders obeyed. In view of this an urban uprising in its ideal state is all but impossible to succeed.

In fact an urban uprising will usually only occur in conjunction with a general insurgent assault on that town or city, after a protracted guerrilla campaign has weakened the government. The example of the military disaster of the Tet offensive has already been given, but there are two others worth mentioning: the failure of the communist guerrillas in their assault on San Salvador in 1989, and the success of the Sandinistas in 1979. This later case was only achieved following the withdrawal of US support for the Samoza government. In fact setting up the United Front was almost all that it took to sweep the Sandinistas into power. However it is interesting to note that, its nature having become known, the Sandinista government was voted out once democratic elections were finally allowed in 1990.

There have been occasions when something like an urban uprising has succeeded, such as Moscow in 1991, Buenos Aires in 1982, or in Tunisia and Egypt in 2011, but these cases were marked by a collapse of the government rather than the power of the people. It usually happened that the soldiers, the main prop of the government, showed signs of sympathy with the insurgents and the generals passed on warnings and advice to the rulers. In fact it is common for the army to step in and stage a coup, 'to preserve order'.

It can be seen, then, that the party planning an uprising has plenty of preparatory work to do. This period is similar to the political phase of Communist Revolutionary Warfare and has the aim of creating a government-in-waiting. Intensive political work will be carried out among key groups of workers, such as railwaymen or communications technicians so that the government's response to the uprising, such as troop movements, may be frustrated at the critical moment. Also it is important that the trade unions should obey the new government after it has seized power. This period will see some selective terrorism and politically based crime, but not random terrorism designed to keep the population on edge. This will seldom help the insurgents' cause. There will be plenty of strikes, riots and demonstrations. They are necessary to remind the authorities and, more importantly the people, that there is a struggle in progress. Finally propaganda must be carefully handled. Cities are covered with advertising and revolutionary propaganda must stand out from this.

The consequences of not fully preparing for a rising may be read in any history of the Paris Commune. Conversely the Russian October revolution showed the results of careful planning. Once any semblance of power has been achieved the revolutionaries must drive on ruthlessly to consolidate their position. As Friederich Engels wrote: *"The defensive is the death of every armed uprising; it is lost before it measures itself with its enemies"*. It is obvious, then, that the army is very important.

To consider the possible attitude of the army it will be useful to briefly look at the Tsar's army in 1917 and the Kaiser's army in 1918. Both armies were large, numbered in millions, both had been defeated in war and were 'demob happy', and both would be called upon to defend their respective regimes, and both failed. Both armies tended to just fall apart as the returning regiments reached their base depots. Such units as did retain their cohesion refused to fight against their countrymen, and were easily swayed by propaganda and contact with civilians. But units of soldiers were necessary. In Russia the Bolsheviks used Lettish troops loyal to them to carry them to power by driving out other members of the Constitutional Assembly. A necessary measure as the Bolsheviks never had a democratic majority. Despite later propaganda the Winter Palace was stormed not by crowds of fervent revolutionary workers but by about 200 disciplined troops.

The German experience was more interesting. Following the armistice a Communist revolution seemed to be sweeping across the industrial cities and the conscript army was useless to stop it. However as the troops disbanded themselves they left behind a small core of soldiers – desperadoes, adventurers or heroes, depending on one's point of view – who were to form the *Freikorps*, and later the armed SA, and enabled the government to put down, often very brutally, the attempted revolution.

The coup and the uprising mark the extremes of the range of this type of insurgency. The most important parameter of this range is public involvement. This can depend to some extent on the degree of development of the state structure. Some post-colonial states, particularly in Africa, have had such poor state structures that there was little to prevent coup after coup. Conversely as the state structure has been better developed it is found that public employees tend to be loyal to the government which, after all, pays their wages. This means that coups are more difficult and require much more public involvement and, ultimately, fighting as they take on the characteristics of an uprising.

A coup in its purest form will only affect the ruling circle and will leave the rest of the population untouched, and, most importantly will not provide any causes for warfare. As the insurrection becomes more public so after it there will be a greater feeling of discontent among the population as a whole and especially among émigrés, the number of whom will increase. After an insurrection the new government is very vulnerable. It has antagonised a portion of the population and has made over-blown promises to the rest who will inevitably feel some degree of disillusion. There may be tensions between various factions and classes that might result in fighting. Against this background decisive action by *émigrés*, particularly if they can call on foreign backing, may seem to have a chance of success. However experience from the French and Russian revolutions through to the Bay of Pigs shows that counter-strokes by *émigrés* are very unlikely to succeed, but rather tend to rally support to the new government.

Should the insurrection fail its supporters will be hunted down by the security forces. The population in general will have little time for them. Most will become fugitives in the countryside, but some will try to hold out in the towns regarding themselves as urban guerrillas. Their case will become steadily more desperate until they become merely criminals shouting political slogans, and terrorists.

The descriptions of the foregoing cases, countryside and city based insurgencies, have, with the exception of Malaya, assumed a homogeneous insurgent population, and that the aim of the insurgent government is to induce the entire population to rise against the government. The situation is complicated dramatically when there are racial divisions within the country which have resulted in bitter enmity. Then one racial group, feeling oppressed in some way, will initially protest against the government. This will bring it into conflict with the remainder of the population. The government may try to be totally even-handed in its dealings with all races, but inevitably will end up relying on one.

If the insurgent race constitutes the majority of the population then events will progress as above, but if it is a minority then the government can only try to placate it by redressing the complained of wrong. If this does not result in the emergency blowing itself out then the situation will result in either partition or 'ethnic cleansing'. Which is to say that the minority will either achieve a place of its own or will be driven out. Both of these alternatives are desperate measures, both result in widespread population movement. Partition will polarise the population ultimately resulting in ethnic cleansing, and ethnic cleansing without partition will result in a refugee problem of colossal proportions. Either will be pregnant with problems for the future.

The Security Forces

The previous two sections of this chapter have considered sub-conventional warfare largely from the insurgent's point of view. This section will summarise the actions undertaken by the security forces, which can include the police, gendarmerie, army and other armed services, and militia. The gendarmerie is a force half-way between police and army. It is armed sufficiently for a heavy skirmish, but not for a protracted battle.

The usual peacetime situation is that law and order are maintained by the police. In a highly civilized country this is done by the unarmed 'bobby on the beat', and the more similar the bobby is to the local population the more effective he will be. Unfortunately in many developing countries the police force is regarded as little better than an occupying army, and one that treats the people with contempt. The further away policing is from the bobby on the beat model the more vulnerable the country may be to an insurgency.

An insurgency may be said to have started when the police and gendarmerie can no longer cope with the level of violence. Then the government will send in some military units 'in Support of the Civil Power'. Initially the troops will come under police control and will undertake basically defensive tasks: guards and escorts, riot policing, local patrolling, observation post manning, and check point and vehicle control point manning.

Soon more aggressive actions will be called for, like house searches and arrests. These actions are usually the results of tip-offs from the public. These must be acted on as soon as possible, or this source of intelligence will dry up. As the scale of these kinds of operations increases so the military units will start to function independently of the police, but still with the co-operation of police intelligence and Special Branch.

If the insurgency is so far progressed that liberated areas have been set up the army will attack them as soon as it feels ready. Having occupied them the government's presence must be made permanent, so defended posts must be set up and garrisoned. This naturally is an extra load for the troops as supply convoys to these posts will be targeted by the insurgents and must be escorted.

If the action is taking place in a rural area the liberated areas can be assumed to lie along the national border, so the border must be closed, a further commitment for the army. The inevitable result is that most of the soldiers are tied down in defensive tasks. During the Soviet-Afghan War usually around 75% of Soviet troops were occupied like this. This figure actually peaked at 85%, and this despite the fact that the Soviet troops carried out most of the offensive operations with Afghan troops doing guards.

Whenever there are troops and transport available the army will organise sweeps and cordon and search operations in the countryside, and house searches in the towns. These seldom net guerrillas or find weapons, but accompanying intelligence personnel should conduct interviews, in private, with as many people as possible to build up the intelligence picture. Ideally, but not that often possible, observation posts will be set up to maintain the government's presence.

The aim of these operations is to be able to contain the insurgency indefinitely at a minimal cost. In towns this will involve setting up a network of informers and getting the police back on the streets. In open country some sort of government paid irregular militia should be set up. These units can be based on the population in general, as in the case of the already mentioned Kikuyu Guard, on ex-servicemen or on insurgents who have changed sides. The best examples of the latter type of unit were the Ferquats (pronounced 'ferkers') of turned insurgents set up by the Omani army during the Dhofar war of the late 1960s and early 1970s.

However, no matter how good police and militia are, the army must make it its absolute priority to attack relentlessly any full-time guerrilla units, and not expect the other forces to do this.

Prompt and violent action by the troops can often have a major impact even if not that successful tactically. In 1978 an Egyptian air liner was hijacked and landed in Cyprus. A plane load of Egyptian special forces was sent to recapture it. The result was a fiasco which caused the deaths of fifteen of these men, but the Egyptian government had shown that it would fight and no more Egyptian air liners were hijacked.

In this context the words of General Wolfe, the Hero of Quebec, are worth considering:

"The loss of a thousand men is rather an advantage to a nation than otherwise, seeing that gallant attempts raise its reputation........ whereas the contrary appearances sink the credit of a country, ruin the troops, and create infinite uneasiness and discontent at home."

So far the armed forces have been assumed to be of the same nationality as the country's government, but there have been many cases when this was not so. Naturally during the period of European empires the army was that of the imperial power, but that period is now passed. However in the post-imperial world this situation keeps recurring, most notably with US troops in Vietnam and Soviet troops in Afghanistan. In these cases as the war winds down, so the foreign troops are replaced by native ones, usually trained up by the foreign army for the task, what the Americans called 'Vietnamisation'. How successful this is will be shown by the post-war history of the countries involved.

Armies are often called on to produce and disseminate propaganda, mostly because they are the only organisations available at the time capable of doing this. This is not usually a good use of soldiers. Propaganda coming from the army is less credible than that from the civil government, and producing it can lead the army into politics which may have bad results. However the security forces in general must never forget the potential importance of political action which, in it succeeds in influencing public opinion, can cause the flow of recruits for the guerrillas to dry up.

For soldiers counter-insurgency is really boring and frustrating. It is easy for the troops, under the pressure of the hatred whipped up against them, and losses suffered by continual small scale actions, to carry out atrocities. Torture and intimidation can seem sensible in the short term, but never in the long. Discipline must be maintained and the troops not allowed to run amok. In this respect the British

Army's policy in Northern Ireland of short, four month, tours of duty was sensible in the long term, as troops serving a short tour were less likely to vent their frustration on the local population.

The Military Revolt

So far this chapter has considered sub-conventional warfare as being between the government and the people. This section will consider the case of the armed forces conspiring against the government.

It is not surprising that such a clash should take place, the armed forces are naturally the most powerful part of the social system but, as the mention of the Kapp *Putsch* has shown, it is not always easy to convert military force into political power. To do this becomes more difficult the more highly developed is the state.

A military revolt can take the form of a coup, an urban rising or a civil war. The Spanish Civil War grew out of the partial success of a military revolt. Inevitably states that fight few external wars are the most likely to experience military revolts, and the large number of military governments round the world shows how common the phenomenon is.

Among the stable European countries, since 1945 there has been little armed forces involvement in politics although in certain countries, like Spain, the opinions of the forces are always respected. In Portugal the Army took a major part in the upheavals following the resignation of the dictator Antonio de Oliveira Salazar in 1968 following a stroke. The Army was demanding, and achieved, an end to the Portuguese wars in Africa. In 1961 there was a mutiny of French forces, mostly Foreign Legion paratroop battalions, in Algeria protesting against the government's policy towards the Algerian war. It was known as the *'Generals' putsch'*. This rising quickly crumbled. Apart from these cases, and coups in Greece and Turkey, civil power has reigned supreme.

Before 1939 the loyalty, or otherwise, of its forces was a matter of great concern to the National Socialist government of Germany. As Adolf Hitler's socialist policy became apparent the services showed what was to become a common reaction. The Air Force was for the socialist government. The Navy was conservative, sceptical but obedient, and the army was sitting on the fence. The Fuhrer tried to use his Storm Troops, the SA, as a militia to deter opposition from the army, but they became too left-wing and almost revolutionary in spirit, so he emasculated the SA in the 'Night of the Long Knives'. He then started to build up the SS.

In a less developed country a government which tries to introduce socialist measures, no matter how well meaning, will clash with the army. Senior officers are frequently big land owners, or are from land owning families, and will see the government as a threat. The government has three methods of countering military hostility. It can, in effect, bribe the forces with high pay and quality equipment. It can try to keep a tighter control of the army, although this will usually result in it being less militarily effective, which is a little self-defeating. The situation in South Vietnam in the early 1960s illustrated this well. Military coup followed military coup in Saigon while the Viet Cong made steady gains in the countryside. The image of tanks crashing into the grounds of the Presidential Palace was a strong very one and was probably on Prime Minister Harold Wilson's mind when, in an angry exchange of words, he told a trade unionist to "*get your tanks off my lawn.*"

The third way of countering military hostility is to follow the SA route and set up some kind of workers' militia outside the military hierarchy and loyal to the government. As will be seen this worked in Cuba where the militia took a part in defeating the Bay of Pigs landing, but in Argentina Juan

Peron would not set one up as he feared he would become its political prisoner. A decision he presumably later regretted.

Juan Peron was elected as the President of Argentina in 1946. Although prior to this date he had been a part of the ruling military junta, he developed a power base among trades unionists, depending on their ability to mobilise mobs of many thousands at short notice. It was inevitable that he would not be popular with the armed forces.

In order to secure his position and reduce hostility from the forces Peron increased military spending. The armed forces, which included the National Police, consisted of 200,000 men, a not unreasonable number of a population of 17,000,000, were well paid and well equipped. This allayed military opposition for a time. He also increased public spending in other areas, this resulted in a high rate of inflation. Worse, a series of bad harvests caused food shortages. However his personal popularity remained high, largely due to his extreme nationalism. However when he initiated an anti-clerical campaign and his Peronista mobs began burning churches some senior military and naval men decided he had to go.

The first attempt occurred in 1951, but it was badly prepared. The insurgents tried to seize a battalion of thirty tanks, but the NCOs of the unit prevented them. After that failure the conspirators had no chance.

A more serious attempt came in June 1955. The leader was Admiral Toranzo who was the Marine Corps Chief of Staff. His plan was simple, to bomb and storm the seat of government, the Casa Rosada, in Buenos Aires with a view to killing or capturing the President. He had wide spread backing in the Navy but little in the Army. He planned for the rising to start on 16th June, but postponed it at the last moment. Unfortunately news of the postponement did not reach all the conspirators and at the originally appointed time some of the staff and students at a school for NCOs commandeered some civilian buses and proceeded in the Casa Rosada. They must have been a little uneasy when they realised that other planned actions were not happening. They were not joined by various Marine units, the radio station had not been seized, and no planes were bombing the Casa Rosada. The Commandant of the school, not being in on the secret, raised the alarm and tried to arrest some of the conspirators.

Following this rather inauspicious start some rebel units decided to join the rising. Some training aircraft tried to attack the Casa Rosada. They made little impression on the population in general which was expecting an air display on that day, and little impression on Peron who was being sheltered by a loyal army unit. Rather belatedly some retired officers seized the radio station but their transmissions were quickly cut off.

The critical action was that of the 4th Marine Battalion. It occupied the Naval HQ then marched on the Casa Rosada, only a short distance away. Unfortunately the government had had time to summon some loyal army units. There was an intense battle before the marines surrendered. That was at around 4pm. Some actions spluttered on a little longer but, really, the conspiracy had failed. It failed because of poor co-ordination. Many naval, and some army, units would have joined had it looked as if it were succeeding. It cost around a thousand casualties, mostly civilian.

Following the failure of the June *putsch* the Peron government took steps to reduce the Navy's capacity for coups, such as bringing the issue of ammunition under government control and reducing the number of marine battalions. These measures did not mollify the Navy's basic anti-Peron stance. However the end of the Peron regime was brought about by the Army.

On 1st September 1955 a unit in Cordoba declared against Peron. Cordoba is about 440 miles west of Buenos Aires.

The government miscalculated and did not take this apparently minor action seriously. In fact the rising was not making any headway until, fourteen days later, a senior retired general, General Lonardi, called in and placed himself at its head. As General Lonardi was dying of cancer he had little to lose, but with a high profile figurehead the rising expanded quickly. Its strategy was, instead of a direct assault on the Casa Rosada, to build up a power base in Cordoba, win over the Navy and Air Force, then mount conventional operations against Buenos Aires.

The plan worked quite well. The Navy quickly joined the revolt, the Air Force proved more difficult. These services followed the usual pattern of the Navy being conservative in sympathy and against the socialist government and the Air Force being in sympathy with it. The Navy, before being really ready for such an action, tried to blockade the Rio de la Plata, the River Plate, with two destroyers. These ships were successfully attacked and driven off by loyal Air Force units flying Gloster Meteors, and their crews sustained heavy casualties. It is possible that the success of this action against warships contributed to the Argentinian decision to concentrate their attacks against British warships during the Falklands War, when targeting supply ships would have been more sensible.

While the conspirators' support in the Navy was increasing, loyalist troops were attacking Cordoba. Once again armoured units had stayed loyal to Peron, but tanks are not at their best in built-up areas. In general loyalist troops did not fight very hard.

Soon the Navy was in a position to try again to blockade the Rio de la Plata. This time it threatened to bombard Buenos Aires. This fact, together with the increasing support for the rising, convinced Peron to renounce the Presidency.

This concluded the Armed Forces vs Government fighting, but the future for Argentina would see a good deal of unrest, *coups* and *putsche*. Juan Peron became a focus for generally socialist anti-government sentiment and, though in exile, was an important person in Argentina until his death.

The Argentinian experience may be more extreme than most, but it is difficult to see why, across the world, the future should see any reduction in the number of military revolts.

Terrorism

No consideration of sub-conventional warfare can ignore terrorism. Since the attack on the World Trade Centre (11th September 2001) terrorism has almost dominated world news coverage and yet there have been surprisingly few attempts to understand the phenomenon of terrorism as opposed to its individual manifestations. The initial problem is simply to define terrorism, particularly as incumbent governments tend to label all insurgents as terrorists. No one definition is generally accepted but for the sake of this study terrorism will be taken as a mode of operation undertaken by an insurgent group involving the carrying out of actions, usually aimed at killing people, the purpose of which is the effect they have on public opinion, rather then the practical result. The target is still the enemy's government but the aim is to influence it via public opinion and, to a lesser extent, through its humanitarian feelings.

There are other modes of action that terrorism might be confused with, being guerrilla warfare, political violence, and politically based crime. In fact a particular event might not fall exactly into one of these classifications but may take on the characteristics of two or three of them.

For example:

> Killing a policeman as a part of an operation aimed at wiping out a police post would be a guerrilla action.
> Killing a policeman as a reprisal for the execution of a

political prisoner would be political violence.

Killing a policeman in the middle of town while he was on ordinary police duty would be terrorism.

Killing a policeman during the course of a bank raid would be a politically based crime.

As can be seen none of these categories is water-tight, but the principle is there that terrorism is not directly an act of war, in fact it is almost a negation of war, but an attempt to manipulate public opinion. It will be seen that terrorist organisations do not evolve through the same stages as military organisations, in fact they are very seldomly capable of any development.

Insurgent organisations usually only initiate a terrorist campaign as a last resort when other methods have been tried. Their recourse to terror can seem like an act of desperation, the only way to protest on a large scale about their various grievances. In many cases the very act of the government including the terror-sponsoring sub or extra-national government in serious consultation or negotiation, will, by reducing the frustration of powerlessness, cause the terrorism to fade away. But not always. Terrorism, like many forms of violence, can so easily become a way of life.

When an insurgent organisation consists of a range of terrorists, from the millennial type to the more practical, then negotiations might succeed in splitting them and causing them to fight among themselves. In this context to lump all such people together under the heading of 'terrorists' can be self defeating.

The type of campaign run by the terrorists will vary with their aim. If the terrorists' aim is limited to changing a particular government policy they will try spectacular random atrocities. This type of campaign is often run by proxy by the government of one country against the government of another. For example, the Spanish sent some troops to Iraq as a part of the occupying force. This evoked a terrorist atrocity, in 2004, when a train was blown up killing a hundred and ninety-one people. Rather than face this kind of terrorism the Spanish withdrew their troops from Iraq. Terrorism is used in this way by extra-national organisations, most notably Al Qaeda.

To this category might be added kidnapping and hostage taking, though they might be better termed as political crimes. The most spectacular such actions were a series of aircraft hijackings in 1970 carried out by the Popular Front for the Liberation of Palestine. They were very successful in the short term.

A proxy terror campaign may well be carried out by what is usually called a 'fifth column'. The most significant fifth column of the last century was that of the Sudeten Germans who caused general unrest and general insecurity before the German occupation of that district. Since then the threat of fifth columns has usually been grossly over-estimated. However in the age of unrestricted immigration this might change.

If the terrorists want to replace the government they will have to mount a protracted campaign of murder and other atrocities the end of which can be difficult to predict. The terrorists will select victims that would not be targets in real war and this very unpredictability make any pattern of terrorist actions difficult to discern. However there is a very tenuous one based on the scale of apparent randomness of targets. At one end of this scale the victims will often be members of the ruling establishment, but certainly not always. Unpredictability is more important than deadliness. As the scale of randomness increases booby traps may be laid, or bombs thrown, at shops, restaurants and other places that members of the establishment visit. If the ruling elite comes from a minority racial group then the markets and streets in their area may be targeted. Finally bombs could be exploded in population centres totally randomly. The purpose of all this is to show that the government cannot cope and hence is not really legitimate.

Attacks on the security forces will attempt to cause them to over-react, run amok and carry out atrocities of their own. This will discredit both them and the government.

The degree of randomness of terrorist actions may be related to the degree of sympathy for the terrorist cause shown by the population in general. As the population is less sympathetic, so the terrorists' actions will be higher up the scale of randomness. At the height of randomness the terrorist is trying to create a situation that people will want to end even if this can only happen by the terrorist gaining power, or the government acceding to his wishes.

Also the degree of randomness may change during a terrorist campaign. At the start a campaign may be very focussed, but as the security forces improve and 'legitimate targets' become less vulnerable, so the campaign may become more random. The alternative will be for the campaign to fade away.

The obvious actions are undertaken against the government, but probably the most important type of terrorism is that aimed at intimidating the public. Critics and political opponents will be beaten up or killed and a hate campaign directed against them, usually with graffiti and posters. To demonstrate their control of the population the terrorists will order such things as a general strike, or all shops to close on a particular day, and anyone not heeding the call will be in trouble. Similarly the terrorists will ensure that the security forces, their families and all government personnel are ostracised, even though this will mean loss of business for many tradesmen.

Taken to its theoretical limit, with total control of the population the terrorist organisation will become the real government. The people will obey it and the incumbent government, which has already shown itself unable to cope, will become irrelevant. Finally the terrorist organisation will be internationally recognised as the government. It is true that no terror campaign has worked quite this neatly, but some in Central and South America have come close.

If the terrorist organisation becomes the national government, it will still retain its grip on its population. This will become an example of state terrorism, as discussed in the next section.

Finally there are terrorist organisations whose aims can only be describes as Millennial. Some, like the anti-capitalist Baader-Meinhof group in Germany, or the Symbionese Liberation Army in the USA, had vague plans to bring the 'whole guilty temple' down with a few murders. Some Muslim radicals have declared war on the whole world, to make everyone a potential target in their campaign to set up the perfect Islamic state, '*Dar ul-Islam*'. One of the Provisional IRA's aims is the creation of '*Eire Nua*', which requires the setting up of a totally Gaelic Ireland, insulated from any contact with England. Unfortunately increased US and EU influence in the Republic make this seem silly.

Millennial groups, like those mentioned here, in the long run are not very important, and there is little point in trying to negotiate with them.

Terrorism seldom exists in a vacuum, but will normally form a part of a wider strategy, and this may further affect the type of terror employed. If the insurrection is taking the form of a guerrilla war of the Communist Revolutionary Warfare type only government personnel and opposition politicians will be targeted. If the aim is for an urban uprising then there could be a sudden outbreak of random terrorism to set the population on edge. Similarly such an outbreak could precede a *coup d'état,* so that the people will welcome the coup if only to end the violence.

The essence of terrorism is publicity, consequently the best defence against it would be to ignore it and let the police treat it as an ordinary crime. This unfortunately is not a viable option in a democracy because the free press and other media, which are a feature of democracy, will naturally sensationalise terrorist actions. This is the real reason why terrorism is much more effective in democratic societies than in totalitarian ones where the governments control the media. Publicity is also the reason why there is a general reluctance to negotiate with terrorists. The incumbent government has usually run a propaganda campaign denouncing the terrorists in the bluntest terms, so just to be seen speaking to them would involve a substantial climb down. However there are times when it should be done. For example, at the time of writing, after protracted negotiations the Provisional IRA has abandoned the 'armed struggle' and its leaders have entered legitimate politics.

The Armed forces – People – Government model works for terrorists as it does for conventional societies, though in many terrorist organisations the government and armed forces merge. The active terrorists, operating in very small units (cells), despite their bank raids and arms stealing exploits, are dependent on their supporters in the same way that a regular army depends on the tax payers. This dependence may offer a weak point that the government can attack by exploiting the horror of terrorism and, in effect, asking the terrorists' supporters if they really want to continue with that sort of thing. In general they do. For example Al Qaeda and its supporters were very satisfied with the attack on the World Trade Centre. However when the victims are more similar to the terrorists this approach can work. It seems to have done so in Northern Ireland where it could be that the greater availability of good quality televisions has brought home the nature of terrorist actions.

There is a great difference between a small terrorist organisation and an urban guerrilla unit, even if the difference is not obvious and of only academic interest to the security forces. The terrorists must operate in cells making as little contact with the public as possible so as to avoid the police. Consequently they become progressively inward-looking and elitist and finally develop a contempt for the mass of the people who are not judged worthy of them. At the same time their aims become more fantastic, like the almost mystical '*Eire Nua*' of Irish dissidents. The result of this is that although they might not be captured it is likely that they will become remote from the real world and will lose their political credibility. Conversely the urban guerrillas, if they are not to fade away, must gain credibility by expanding their power base, but doing this results in their vulnerability, and usually downfall.

In short pure terrorism falls outside the scope of the study of war but this is not obvious to most of the world's media, and concepts like 'War against Terror' are not viable.

It is impossible to give an instance of a successful campaign based purely on terrorism, though Aden (1964-1967) came close. The difficulty is caused by the shortage of good quality published information. This shortage is partly due to the clandestine nature of the subject, but it is likely to be mostly due to the squalid nature of terrorism, which makes it difficult to feel proud of it afterwards. There can be little doubt that the bulk of the success gained by the IRA in the Anglo-Irish war was achieved by terror, which may well be why no good history of that war has yet been published. A brief consideration will be given here to the conflict in Cyprus, which, if not a perfect example of a terror campaign, is as good as any.

Britain occupied Cyprus in 1878, but never showed much interest in it. By the 1950s it was only important for its airfields and its radar and radio stations. The population is largely Greek (415,000) with a Turkish minority (105,000). In 1954 the island had just been made the location of the Middle East Headquarters, with a garrison of two battalions. During the years up to 1955 a political movement grew up among the Greek Cypriots demanding union with Greece,

'*Enosis*'. This movement, which naturally had no appeal for the Turkish minority, was led by Archbishop Makarios. In command of the fighting units was Colonel (retired) Grivas. Grivas set up a number of small units operating from safe houses in the countryside. They could carry out small scale raids, but no more. This force was called 'EOKA'. The term is an acronym for the Greek for National Organisation of Cypriot Fighters.

The insurrection started in April 1955, proceeding with a series of attacks on police stations and grenade and bomb attacks on army accommodation and bars used by troops. These were followed by rioting. The greater part of the EOKA effort was put into coercing the Greek population into supporting the insurrection, and attacking the police. Most of the policemen killed were Turkish. As a consequence of all this the Turkish population became restless and started to demand the partition of Cyprus. The garrison was reinforced with four battalions and finally reached a total of 40,000 troops.

The reinforced troops soon made the countryside too hot for EOKA, but Grivas was an efficient and ruthless terrorist. He knew that the insurgency would be won or lost in the towns. He controlled the population through intimidation but he went one step further, he radicalised school children with a propaganda campaign, knowing that protesting school children being controlled, or as it would be reported, repressed by British troops would make good copy. This radicalisation of school children was Grivas's most successful policy. He was helped by a mistaken government policy in what he called 'the Battle of the Flags'. On EOKA's orders the schools flew Greek flags, and the troops were ordered to take them down. This resulted in many children's riots. It would have been better to have left them alone.

In November a State of Emergency was declared with provisions for extending the death penalty and inflicting collective punishments of curfews and fines. As things got worse the British decided to remove the leadership of the insurgency by exiling Makarios. This was a policy that worked well in other countries, but unfortunately in Cyprus it only had the effect of leaving Grivas in control. Makarios, despite his anti-Britishness, was realistic in being prepared to accept independence without Enosis. Grivas fanatically demanded *Enosis*. Probably fortunately for international relations neither Greece nor Turkey was interested in Cyprus or EOKA.

Grivas and EOKA continued to goad the troops by frequent small scale attacks, but their greatest success came after the murder of a soldier's wife and attacks on others. This did cause an over-reaction, and in the subsequent round up over 200 people were beaten up and two died in custody, one by a heart attack, the other violently. This caused the British public, which so far had been indifferent to Cyprus, to grow uneasy. This spurred the government to release Makarios and grant independence, but not *Enosis*. Makarios became the first president of Cyprus. Britain did quite well out of this, retaining two large bases for a reasonable rent, and being relieved of the expense of governing the island.

Enosis was ruled out by the constitution, and the complex voting system, of the new state, and more importantly by Greece and Turkey not wanting it. Even so the distrust between the Greek and Turkish Cypriots would not die down and actually increased in 1964 when Grivas returned to Cyprus to lead the party calling for *Enosis*. This party received a considerable boost in 1967 when the Greek Colonels staged a successful *coup d'état*, but even so official Greek policy towards Cyprus did not change.

Finally Grivas and EOKA decided that Mararios had to go and in 1974 staged a coup against him. There is a hint of irony in that, after all his anti-British activities, he was glad to be able to reach the safety of a British base. He was replaced by Nikos Sampson, an EOKA man.

While this was happening, the Turkish government, observing that *Enosis* was now more likely and, not wanting a potentially hostile island so close to their shore, invaded Cyprus and partitioned the island. This resulted in many more Greek Cypriots seeking sanctuary in British bases. Cyprus has remained partitioned ever since. Makarios was soon reinstated as president.

The EOKA campaign killed 99 security forces personnel, including 21 police, both British and Cypriot. Around 70 EOKA personnel were killed. There were also civilian deaths resulting from EOKA's intimidation of the population and fighting between the Greek and Turkish Cypriot communities. The scale of these casualties is hinted at by the discovery, in September 1974, of a mass grave containing the remains of 60 Turkish Cypriots.

It is difficult to believe that the end result could be called a success for EOKA. The aim of EOKA was *Enosis* and this did not happen. Makarios would settle for an independent Cyprus, which he got, but it was unstable and this inevitably resulted in partition. The conclusion must be that it would have been better for Cyprus if the campaign had not taken place. The British would have granted independence quite soon, there would have been no inter-community strife, no partition and the country would have turned into a wealthy tourist paradise.

The EOKA campaign and its aftermath form a parallel with the Anglo-Irish war. In both cases, due to geography and population a campaign of terror was the only realistic tactical option. But terror campaigns result in political aims becoming extreme and inflexible. Once such a campaign has started it is difficult for the insurgent government to exert real control over the terrorist organisation, which inevitably starts to carry the insurgent government with it. This can be seen in Palestine up to the end of the British Mandate, in Algeria, and in Aden where the insurgence degenerated into a civil war between the Front for the Liberation of Occupied South Yemen (FLOSY) and the National Liberation Front (NLF). The difference between these organisations may seem arcane to the outsider. In all these cases the apparently successful conclusion of a terror campaign did not result in a stable and lasting peace.

In the end the whole EOKA phenomenon seems little more than an extension of the egotism of its leader, Grivas. He styled himself as Dighenis, a legendary Greek hero, his autobiography contains passages of total fantasy, and he was indifferent to other people's lives. Such men do not tend to value democratic debate.

State Terrorism

If pure terrorism seems to be outside the study of war then state terrorism is even more so even though it has claimed many more lives than pure terrorism over any period and by any method of accounting. There are three main manifestations of state terrorism.

The first is a violent maintaining of the *status quo*. All reasonably advanced societies depend, to one degree or another, upon inequalities between their members. In the final analysis these inequalities have to be maintained by force. This may involve restraining protesting crowds or even firing on them. As George Orwell commented, '*People sleep peaceably in their beds at night only because rough men stand ready to do violence on their behalf*'. However when a government, in ordering its police and armed forces to apply this force, no longer has the backing of the population as a whole to do this then this force may be termed 'state terrorism', and this violence is often taken as the justification for the violence of the terrorist.

The second is the way in which dissidents or sections of society that may be a threat to the government in any way are intimidated or destroyed. In the case of individuals this often happens through the medium of show trials, or they might be quietly murdered. If the problem is with a large number of people they might be relocated *en bloc*.

The third is the brutal method by which a government enforces its orders on its people. For example peasants living on a site required by the government might be forcibly removed or driven away.

From the point of view of the people there is very little difference between these three cases, they all result in fear and uncertainty. This is the same for a fully entrenched government, like that of Stalinist Russia, as it is for a small insurgent organisation, like EOKA, ensuring obedience among its limited following and the population in general.

As has been shown in the previous section, the terrorists of EOKA cowed the Greek Cypriot population by murders and beatings. Ideally the victims would have been real informers and the like, but often they were picked almost at random, and lies told about them. The effect on the people was the same. It is, though, only a short term fix and generally speaking in the long term it will tend to breed resentment against the terrorists unless the movement can develop to have its armed forces separate and subordinate to its government which has the backing of the people.

There are two ways in which state terrorism is relevant to the study of war. One is an indirect one and is based on the fact that in most countries in the world the state of war is distinct from peace and much worse. In some countries and societies where obedience to the government is enforced by terrorism then war, by displacing state aggression from the people to foreigners, can actually be preferable to peace, and may result in very repressed states being very bellicose.

The other is that state terrorism is a common counter-insurgency technique, and the depressing thing is that it usually works, both in the short term and the long. The most notable example of state terrorism in Great Britain has been the 'Bloody Assizes' following Monmouth's rebellion of 1685. Around 200 men were executed and many more transported. The areas affected were remarkably quiescent three years later during the 'Glorious Revolution'.

In El Salvador the dictator Maximiliano Hernandez Martinez, who seized power in a coup in 1931, suppressed a communist inspired insurgency extremely brutally one year later. In the 1970s and 1980s when revolutionary warfare raged over large tracts of the country the areas where Martinez's men had been most active remained quiet.

There are almost endless such examples. The effectiveness of the atrocities is based on the public's reaction to them and, very occasionally, they can cause a wave of anti-government feeling and be counter-productive.

One of the most notable cases of this occurring was the 'Amritsar Massacre' of 1919. At that time there was a great degree of unrest in the Punjab and a general outbreak of anti-British violence was expected. A British soldier and four civilians, three of whom were bank officials, had been murdered and a British woman attacked and left for dead. Things seemed to be coming to a head when a large crowd gathered in an enclosed area near the centre of Amritsar. The commander of the troops in the area, General Dyer, decided to break up this crowd and ordered 25 Baluchi and 25 Gurkha soldiers to fire into it. They did so with such effect that they killed 379 and wounded around 1,200. The result was that calm descended on the Punjab and in the short term the action had been a great success.

However Indian nationalists and the British government seized upon it. How much of a filip the independence movement gained from it is open to argument, but the General's career was ended even though he was an excellent soldier and had taken a leading part in the Third Afghan War less than two months after the Amritsar incident.

In 1984 a second Amritsar massacre occurred. Amritsar is central to the Sikh religion and had become a base for agitation for an autonomous Sikh state. To this end a terrorist campaign was building up and the Indian government decided to take decisive action. The insurgents had occupied the Golden Temple which was close to the site of the 1919 massacre. This and the rest of the city were heavily shelled then the Indian army mounted a frontal assault, Op Blue Star. This was successful even if it did result in the deaths of between 300 and 700 of the attacking soldiers and of between 500 and 2,000 civilians, some of whom were innocent pilgrims. The Indian government White Paper is a little vague on the number of casualties. The insurgents were wiped out and peace again descended on the Punjab. This time no general's career was ruined.

But blood will have blood and a few months later Mrs Gandhi, the Indian Prime Minister, was murdered by a Sikh soldier of her bodyguard, and even as late as 2012 an attempt was made, in London, on the life of the general who commander Op Blue Star.

In both of the massacres at Amritsar far more civilians were killed than was necessary to achieve the immediate military purpose. These extra deaths were the result of state terrorism as a means of cowing the population.

In terms of public perception of state terror it is of interest to note how over time the Chinese government has altered its description of the Tiananmen massacre. It was first described as the 'Tiananmen Turmoil', then it became an 'Incident', and it finally became the 'Tiananmen Event'!

The IRA

Many of the aspects of sub-conventional warfare discussed in this chapter were demonstrated during the Anglo-Irish War of 1919 to 1922 and the Northern Irish 'Troubles' of 1967 to 2007. To illustrate these this section will give a brief account of the development of the IRA, its limitations and the difficulties it posed for the Security Forces.

The Anglo-Irish War

The history of the IRA shows how proportionately greater can be the effects of the actions of a small revolutionary hardcore than the numbers of men involved would indicate. These men were members of the Irish Republican Brotherhood (IRB). It is true that this was just one secret society among many others, but it was the most persistent and successful. Its aims for an independent Ireland were of the romantic kind that later morphed into '*Eire Nua*'.

One of the reasons for the success of the IRB, and later of the Irish Republican Army (IRA), was that Ireland has always been a breeding ground for sectarianism and secret societies, something which the English found, and still find, difficult to understand.

The Home Rule bill first went before parliament in 1912, and, to oppose it the Ulster Protestants founded the Ulster Volunteer Force (UVF). To balance this, a few months later, the National Volunteers were founded. The police turned a blind eye to the arming of the UVF, which bought over 24,000 rifles from Germany, but the National Volunteers were prevented from buying a much smaller number.

When the Great War started the National Volunteers were encouraged to enlist in the British Army, but a minority, dominated by IRB members, refused to fight in Britain's war and left the National Volunteers to form the Irish Volunteers.

In 1919 this name was formally changed to the Irish Republican Army, the IRA.

The political party, *Sinn Fein*, which translates roughly as 'ourselves alone', started life in 1905 as a nationalist and pacifist party but, after the Easter Rising, was infiltrated by hardcore IRB-IRA members until it became something like the political wing of the IRA. It is significant that Sinn Fein was never, despite its claims, in control of the IRA.

There are several possible dates for the start of the Anglo-Irish war. The most sensible must be the Easter Rising of 1916. This involved a small number of Irish Volunteers and some others taking over the Dublin GPO and some other buildings, and one of their leaders, Padraig Pearse, reading a Declaration of Irish Independence to some passers-by. If only the Dublin Metropolitan Police, the Royal Irish Constabulary (RIC), and the army had reacted in a low-key fashion the Rising would have degenerated into a farce. Unfortunately they went to the other extreme, mounted a regular siege and a gunboat anchored on the Liffey bombarded the centre of Dublin caused extensive damage. Even so when the rebels surrendered there was little public sympathy for them.

After the rising a large number of the rebels were sentenced to death and 15 actually executed. This was quite reasonable in law, they were guilty of treason and murder, but, as with the execution of Edith Cavell by the Germans, political common sense should have taken precedence over legalities.

These executions started to swing public opinion round to the rebels and Sinn Fein. Two further actions reinforced this trend. The prisoners were released and this hardcore was able to provide the leadership of the insurgency. Secondly there was a plan to extend conscription to Ireland.

The result of all this was that, during the last two years of the Great War membership of the Irish Volunteers dramatically increased and it was organised into local companies and battalions. Also Sinn Fein did very well in the general election of 1918. They won 73 out of 105 seats, but refused to take their seats at Westminster. Instead they convened an Irish parliament, the Dail Eireann, in Dublin. It was not a great success as a functioning body as many of its members were either in jail or on the run, but the important fact was that it existed. From then on the conflict was about which of the two parliaments was the legitimate ruler of Ireland.

The obvious tactic for Sinn Fein to follow was to destroy the RIC. This was not that difficult. In rural areas small numbers of police were quartered in indefensible houses misleadingly called barracks. Initially the police, and their families, were boycotted, then on 21st January 1919, the same day as the Dail was first convened, two policemen were murdered in the course of the theft of some explosives. From then on the number of attacks on the police increased dramatically. This date, as opposed to that of the Easter Rising, is usually taken as the start of the Anglo-Irish war though there had been a number of low level incidents before it.

The IRA was deliberately forcing the pace, feeling a need to establish itself as public enthusiasm was starting to wane. Although publicly Sinn Fein claimed that its election victory was a mandate for war, privately it understood that this just was not the fact, and preferred to move slowly.

As attacks on the RIC increased they abandoned their smaller barracks and concentrated in the larger ones. There had been a large number of resignations from the force. It was largely Catholic and many policemen had a degree of sympathy for the rebels, also the boycott was unpleasant for the families, and, of course there were the casualties. The British government, needing to quickly make up the numbers, recruited reinforcements from ex-soldiers. These were called the 'Blacks and Tans', or just the 'Tans'. Soon after they recruited some ex-officers to make up companies of a type of gendarmerie, the Auxiliary Division RIC, the

'Auxies'. Unfortunately neither the 'Tans' nor the 'Auxies' were real policemen and their behaviour was to have a detrimental effect on public opinion.

The IRA can be said to have developed in the classic way, going from the Aristocratic phase of a few dedicated men to the Militia phase of the local companies to the professional flying columns. The fact that the IRA could not defeat the British militarily does not invalidate this.

As the IRA campaign progressed successfully, the next stage was against the judiciary. Magistrates were driven out, or killed, and the IRA set up its own police and courts to present Sinn Fein as the legitimate government. In this they were only partly successful and the final result was more likely to be lawlessness than Irish law.

Rebel violence followed two distinct trends. In the countryside the regional organisation of companies and battalions was not proving effective. The fighting units did not become strong or proficient enough. The system gave way to flying columns. These came together almost spontaneously from men on the run who became their full time members. They naturally took the greater share of arms and ammunition, thus further reducing the effectiveness of local units, but they still expected the local units to provide supplies, guides, intelligence and safe houses. This could cause friction. The flying columns gave the army something to shoot at, and although they are a major part of Irish legend, they were not that effective and they took the leaders away from the local units where they should have been organising constant sabotage and pin-prick attacks.

The other trend, that in the cities, saw the insurgency start with some major riots and protests, but these quickly gave way to low grade terrorism. In Dublin there was a long-lived and bloody feud between various intelligence units and the IRA, but how important this was in the big picture is hard to gauge.

The British army units were never very effective against the IRA. Their recent experience had been in artillery dominated conventional warfare, they were under strength and just did not know what to do. It would have been most sensible to have placed them directly under RIC control but it seems that this was not seriously considered. The great need was for intelligence and it was only towards the end of the fighting that this problem was being overcome. Remarkably it was found that captured IRA men were the best sources of information, particularly those in local units dragooned into providing assistance for a flying column.

The population in general, particularly in rural areas, soon grew weary of the war. Trains were not running and the roads were perpetually sabotaged. Produce could not reach the markets, and Sinn Fein knew that the war must end soon. So did the British government. Consequently a settlement was found, not that different from that proposed in 1912. This was not accepted by the Protestant north so the result, which was not initially a part of British policy, was partition. When partition was a fact the British government regarded it as only temporary, but large numbers of Protestants moved from the south to the north, some to follow their Civil Service jobs, some because of economic factors – the departure of the British army took many jobs with it, and some because of what must be called the persecution, sometimes to the extent of murder, of Protestants in Catholic Southern Ireland. The result of his population shift has been that the North has been determined ever since never to be reunited with the South.

Mostly because of partition some IRA units did not accept the peace treaty, and its signing was followed by a short civil war which the Pro-Treaty troops quickly won. It is interesting to note that their treatment of prisoners was much more severe than anything managed by the preceding British forces.

It is worth a few lines to consider the attitude of the British government towards Irish independence. Before the Great War the British parliament, if not enthusiastic, did pass the Third Home Rule Bill which allowed a degree of devolution. However its implementation was suspended due to the war. The delay evoked the Easter Rising of 1916. That incident was reasonably regarded as treachery by the British government which was fighting the greatest war the country, and the world, had ever known.

After the war came the Paris Peace Conference. Although the Versailles Treaty was signed in June 1919, the conference continued until January 1920, a year after the start of the Anglo-Irish War. During this time the British government, needing the United Kingdom as a weight in the balance of power, was not going to consider that it might be broken up. Lloyd George ensured that an attempt to have the Irish Republic recognised at Paris came to nothing. After January the existence of the United Kingdom was no longer necessary, even so the government moved slowly, almost as if it refused to take the problem seriously. Ireland has a history of bouts of anarchy and the government seems to have believed that this was just another and it would pass. By November 1920 the Government of Ireland Act was passed. This act called Northern Ireland into existence, but was not workable in the South. After that the government's mind began to change.

By April 1921 the Cabinet was considering negotiation. It was unfortunate that those it was preparing to negotiate with it had previously characterised as 'murderers', but *realpolitik* prevailed. At the time the army was generally optimistic and believed that, with reasonable reinforcements, it could pacify Ireland. The government, though, knew that public opinion was starting to demand an end to the campaign. The unsavoury activities of the Blacks and Tans were well known, and a policy of repression was the opposite of the policy of self-determination for small nations which was supposed to have been what the Great War was fought about.

119

Further the government was worried about the possible effect of the rebellion on Anglo-American relations. Also the requested reinforcements were hard to find. Consequently Lloyd George negotiated, admitting something like defeat, and securing a truce in July 1921, leading to the Treaty of December that year.

There can be no doubt of the strength of British public feeling against the continuation of the campaign. The greatest single influence on public opinion was the Labour Party, and the report of its Commission on Ireland, which was published in January 1921, concluded that *"Things are being done in the name of Britain which must make her name stink in the nostrils of the whole world."*

However a cynic might comment on how easily manipulated public opinion could be. Only two decades, less than a generation, later the public was indifferent to the progress of the Bomber Offensive which, being the systematic massacre of non-combatants, was a much greater atrocity than anything seen in Ireland.

It must be agreed that the government did not handle the crisis well, but throughout the period in question it was extremely busy on the world stage and no doubt it was easy to hope that problems would sort themselves out. It was not helped by the fact that many of the aristocracy and senior army officers described themselves as Anglo-Irish and held large estates in Ireland.

The Provisionals

The end of the Civil War in 1922 was not the end of the IRA. This section will consider its history in the period since 1967. Before this date it had been of steadily declining importance. Those members that were still active still refused to accept the partition of Ireland, and they ran a campaign from 1956 to 1962 which involved little more than making small scale raids across the border into Northern Ireland to attack police stations, or targets such as power stations or bridges. These raids were no more than pin pricks to Northern Ireland, but the IRA was an irritant to the Republic, which took legal action against it and interned large numbers of IRA personnel, as did the Northern Ireland government. Such measures as these, plus tighter security in the north, resulted in the failure of the campaign which fizzled out to public indifference. However it was noted that when IRA men had been killed, their funerals, in the Republic, drew huge crowds and much sympathy. The failure of the campaign resulted in a rethink of basic IRA policy.

In a developed country there is little chance of success in the countryside, so action would have to move to the cities. The problem there was that the majority of the urban population was, and is, Protestant, Loyalist and loathed the IRA. Consequently the IRA leadership tried to change its basic policy away from pure nationalism to one of class-based revolution.

With hindsight it can be seen that this idea was totally unrealistic, but regardless of that it never had a chance as it was overtaken by events. By the 1960s Northern Ireland had become one of the poorest parts of the UK and its big employers, like ship builders and textile manufacturers, were shedding large numbers of staff. The Catholic minority felt, with some justification, that it was being unfairly treated particularly where housing and jobs were concerned. The result was a simmering discontent that spilled over into the 'tricolour riots' of 1964 and the Cromac Square riot of 1966. These were unstructured Catholic/Protestant clashes, but in 1967 there came the Civil Rights movement which, in apparent imitation of the Civil Rights movement in the southern states of America, mounted a number of protest marches and demonstrations. It is interesting, and probably significant, that the tension was building up at the same time as the government of Northern Ireland, under Captain Terence O'Neill, was in the process of liberalising its regime. The Catholics may have thought that this was their chance, and the Protestants may have felt threatened.

These marches soon developed into riots and clashes with the police, the Royal Ulster Constabulary (RUC). Then these riots inevitably turned into inter-sectarian fighting.

On the streets the IRA members realised they had to do something in order to retain any degree of credibility, and the younger and more active members were soon taking a lead in the fighting, defending Catholic areas against Protestant assault. Doing this they started to break away from the rest of the IRA. The result of this was that the IRA split into two; the Officials ('Stickies') and the Provisionals ('Provies' or 'Provos'). The 'Sticky' expression derives from the labels they stuck on their lapels when going on some particular rally. The Officials tried to continue preparing for class war and, in practical terms, soon faded away. The fighting was done almost entirely by the Provisionals.

As the RUC was being swamped by the rioting, British troops were deployed in their support. Initially this deployment was popular among the Catholics, the troops being even-handed. However the fact was that the troops were deployed 'in support of the civil power', and that civil power was already discredited in Catholic eyes. Consequently, partly inevitably and partly because of some bad decisions made by the security forces, this popularity soon faded and large sections of the Catholic population came to see themselves as being in conflict with the British army, and to see the Provisionals as their defenders. Some hint of the bitterness generated is given in Appendix 2.

The rioting stage, which may be compared to the Militia stage of military development, reached a high point with the setting up of 'Free Derry'. The British response was to send more soldiers and to reorganise the Special Constabulary.

The vast majority of soldiers came from the BAOR on four month emergency tours. Their accommodation was often basic at best, and they functioned, at least in theory, in close liaison with the RUC. The weakness of this system was that when its tour ended a unit returned *en bloc* to Germany and the next unit had to familiarise itself entirely from scratch. The attachment of one or two liaison officers did not significantly alter this.

The case of the Special Constabulary is of particular interest. They were termed, for historical reasons the 'B' men because they were originally the 'B' Specials. In the closing days of the Anglo-Irish War a Special Constabulary was raised in Ulster consisting of three classes. 'A' Specials were full-time, 'B' Specials were part-time, and the 'C' class was a reserve. The 'B' men term might have been a parallel with the 'G' men, the detectives of 'G' division of the old Dublin Metropolitan Police. The 'B' men were very efficient, 100% protestant, and were held to have been the main reason for the failure of the 1950s campaign. The full weight of republican propaganda was brought to bear against them, so the British government, which by then was governing Northern Ireland directly, being eager to propitiate the insurgents, disbanded them. They were replaced by the Ulster Defence Regiment (UDR) which was similar to a territorial army (TA) unit. The essence of the change was that the UDR supported the army, whereas the Specials had supported the police.

The unrelenting presence of the army wore the rebellion down. Free Derry was easily reoccupied, riots were better handled and the population started to become sick of the whole thing. Insurgent actions sank to a low level of bombings, booby-traps, mine laying, sniping and murders. They tried to disrupt elections but with little success, and carried out the occasional spectacular, that is large bombs sometimes in England. But it made no difference, the soldiers were still there.

As the end was coming, the bulk of actions were carried out by small units which lived in the Republic and crossed the border briefly to fire a few shots or plant a bomb before scuttling back. There is no doubt that militarily the Provisionals were in a *cul-de-sac*, a fact made more obvious when the Republic, which was now involved in a rather heady Europeanism, abandoned its constitutional claim to the North.

A further disaster for the Provisionals was the World Trade Centre atrocity of 11th September 2001. This resulted in a dramatic reduction of funds coming from the USA as people began to realise the nature of terrorism. The fact that IRA wall paintings had often depicted IRA men and Palestinians mutually involved in 'One Struggle' would not have helped.

A hard core of IRA men has not been pleased by their leaders entering politics and hence growing rich. The result of this has been several splinter groups which have pledged to continue the fight. At least so far these have received little public support.

The obvious main reason for the failure of the Provisionals' military campaign was the sectarian nature of society in Northern Ireland, and that they only appealed to the minority. This in itself is a paradox because, in the final analysis, the soldiers were there to protect the Catholics from the Protestant majority. The Catholics knew this, but could not be seen to break ranks with the Provisionals. A secondary reason was that the Provisionals' lack of any political philosophy other than violence. This meant that they could never have an articulate and believable leader, or figurehead, to put their case to the world.

There are two points about the Northern Ireland troubles that are worth noting. Firstly, because the security forces handled the problem in a low-key, almost constitutional manner, the whole thing took four decades. The Army's deployment was code named 'Op Banner', it ran from August 1967 to 31st July 2007 with 763 military deaths.

Secondly, in every society, particularly every city, there is a large number of young men who are eager to fight and kill people providing they have the opportunity, and the approval of the people. And once the killing starts they will not yield up their guns easily.

6

Conventional Warfare

Almost all countries have conventional forces. These are usually called 'Regular troops' which may be a misnomer, regulars being long-service volunteers, whereas conventional forces can include conscripts. In general sub-national government will not be able to afford conventional forces, and will only be able to when they reach the conventional phase of Communist Revolutionary Warfare. Conventional forces include infantry backed up by AFVs and artillery. There will also be an airforce which may, or may not, be, as in Britain, a separate service. Most countries also have a navy, even if very small.

Conventional wars are not always distinct from sub-conventional ones. Most wars include aspects of both. For example in 2003 US and UK forces easily won a conventional war against a rather second rate Iraqi army and occupied Iraq, but both became engaged in internal security operations, which dragged on for years, against a progressively restless population. In such a case as this, one similar to the Boer War (1899-1902) the sub-conventional phase will be the most important to the indigenous population, whereas the attackers will think of the war in terms of the conventional phase.

What can be achieved by conventional warfare is surprisingly obscure. A consideration of Napoleon's wars will illustrate this. Napoleon is considered by many as the greatest general of all time, and was undeniably the greatest of his age. His method was to invade the enemy's country, destroy his army in a great battle, occupy his capital, and dictate peace terms.

This system worked so well because the victim governments were of the aristocratic '*ancien regime*' type, and were eager to conclude the wars before any unrest was stirred up among their people, particularly as Napoleon was supposedly fighting for Revolutionary France. It is interesting that Napoleon always gave winning public opinion as one of his war aims. However the ravages of the French Army, which had no alternative to supporting itself by foraging on a grand scale, caused a great upsurge of patriotism which the governments could take advantage of. The turning point came when Napoleon invaded Russia. The Russians would not treat when he entered Moscow, they just fought harder. From then on Napoleon was opposing nations with his army, and losing.

Napoleon's downfall came about because each of his wars led to the next. In each peace settlement he was unable, or unwilling, to find a deal that would suit everyone and produce stability.

So after each war his enemies became better and more numerous, and in the end he was defeated and exiled. The cycle of wars was ended by the victorious allies with their magnanimous treatment of the French people.

And that is how it has been ever since. As irritating as it would naturally be for the victors any post-war settlement must be acceptable to the enemy's government and people, and enforcing a regime change to achieve this acceptance is fraught with difficulties. The alternative can only be to garrison the enemy's country and impose martial law which might be gratifying for a short while, but in the longer term will be disastrous.

The great achievement of conventional warfare from 1945 has been to maintain the balance of power in the Cold War. That is, the achievement was not to fight. Even if there was no actual warfare the Cold War was the world's most significant strategic fact up to its end in 1991. The most sensitive confrontation was in Germany where the forces of the super-powers, the Soviet bloc (Warsaw Pact) and NATO (USA and Europe), watched each other and practised warfare, the troops being roughly where the armies had halted in 1945.

The Cold War will be described in a subsequent chapter, here it is enough to note its importance, and to consider two of its remarkable effects. Firstly, it resulted in a great rate of weapons development. Normally this slows down in peacetime, but the Cold War did not allow it to. Secondly the major powers clashed in continual proxy warfare around the globe. A warring state would appeal to one bloc for arms and support, so the other bloc would naturally go to the assistance of the other side. The most important example of this is the Arab/Israeli wars. The result of this military assistance was to reduce the tendency of wars to fade away.

Although at the time it was not obvious, it may be that the Cold War was overall 'a good thing' because the confrontation involved the threat of nuclear weapons. This has had the direct effect of forcing on the super-powers a great need for world stability, and if any war has looked as if it could get out of control the super-powers have stopped it, as Britain and France found in the Suez crisis.

It is interesting to note that when a war has occurred in a part of the world of no interest to the super-powers, and it has been carried out with unsophisticated means, then the super-powers have ignored it. For example in Burundi and Rwanda in the 1990s nearly a million Tutsis and Hutus were killed, often in horrifying circumstances, in an outbreak of inter-racial warfare. The world watched with indifference. Such wars as these in third world countries have a natural tendency to degenerate towards primary warfare and grind on as long as anyone has the energy to continue the killing. For example the Congolese Civil War of 1998-2003 was responsible for between three and four million deaths, mostly due to starvation and disease. Even this horror might be eclipsed by the Sudanese Civil War, ongoing at the time of writing.

Apart from maintaining the Cold War the achievements of conventional warfare have been rather limited.

In the Korean and Iran/Iraq wars huge armies, after impressive manoeuvres and heavy casualties, settled down much where they started, and finally called the war off. Similarly there has been fighting between India and Pakistan. This can be traced back to the messy way British India fell apart at the end of the Raj. The main actions were in 1965 and 1971. The latter was a success for the Indians and led to the creation of Bangladesh. But earlier, in 1962, the Indians had the worse of a clash with the Chinese in the high and cold Karakoram mountains. The Chinese, in their turn, were defeated by the Vietnamese in 1979.

The last of the India/Pakistan wars was the Kargil war of 1999. It was basically a Pakistani incursion across the border into Kashmir. After heavy fighting the Indian troops drove them out. This war is of interest because shortly before it both sides had, or were believed to have had, carried out nuclear tests. Consequently the fighting was not allowed to spread, and it is possible that relations between the two countries may become less confrontational.

Large mechanised task forces, commanded by Soviet officers and crewed by Cubans, were deployed in Ethiopia and Angola, and in both countries saw extensive action. In neither case was the outcome of any advantage to either the USSR or Cuba. These cases will be mentioned again in later chapters.

More impressively conventional forces have been used very successfully to restore the pre-war situations in the Falklands, 1982, and in Kuwait, 1991, after these countries had been occupied by sudden surprise invasions.

But mostly, more than all of these, there have been the Arab/Israeli wars. The first of these, 1947-48, was a result of large scale Jewish immigration into Palestine. By the end of the fighting the bulk of the Palestinian population had been driven out, or killed, and the modern state of Israel brought into existence. So far, from the Jewish point of view, the war had been a great success and the original war aim achieved. Unfortunately it was at the cost of intense Arab hostility, which resulted in continuing minor cross-border violence. Consequently the Israelis, having achieved a lot by a successful war, and wanting to achieve more by the same means, have initiated a series of offensive wars attempting to force their neighbours to leave them alone to live in peace in the country they have stolen. After each war each side had its losses in arms and ammunition made good by either the USA or the USSR so that it could prepare for the next. It is important to note that these wars, which have been very photogenic, have all failed in achieving the Israeli war aims, and what is worse, show no signs of coming to an end.

Obviously this little survey makes no claim to be a list of all post-1945 conventional wars. If it did it would certainly have to include the Bay of Pigs landing, which will be covered in a later chapter, and the 1975 North Vietnamese invasion of South Vietnam, mentioned below, and several more even though in some cases the conventional or otherwise classification is open to argument. Enough, though, has been covered for some tentative conclusions to be drawn.

Conventional forces are trained and equipped to fight other conventional forces. This is in line with the Napoleonic system. It has long been apparent that such fighting is only a means to an end and that end must be a better state of peace than that preceding the fighting. To achieve this the fighting must be very carefully controlled. The pre-1914 concept, held by all nations at that time but most strongly by the Germans, a peculiar negation of Clausewitz's philosophy, was that politics ended when the fighting started. This is no longer appropriate, if it ever was, but naturally any sort of political control is resented by military commanders who regard it as amateurish interference. They would prefer to be set a military problem then be left alone to solve it. This, though, is unlikely to happen in anything less than total war. The grossest example of political control was the way that Fidel Castro, in his role as Commander in Chief, was said to spend many hours each day in an office in Havana micromanaging the activities of the Cuban troops in Angola and Ethiopia, even to the point of locating individual artillery pieces.

For a long time communist governments tried to impose political control by having commissars at most levels of command with political considerations taking precedence over military ones. This system was revoked, in the USSR, in the face of total war, and seems to have faded away elsewhere, but judging by Russian experience in Afghanistan and Chechnya they have not yet got the military/political balance right. Experience in Iraq has shown that the same is true for Britain and the USA.

Politicians will not only force their views on the soldiers but, this being a two-way process, will ask for their opinions and recommendations. For this process to run smoothly and with mutual confidence the politicians and the generals must be of similar intellect and social class, as was discussed in Chapter 2. If mutual confidence is achieved a sensible use of force should follow.

Political control is of particular importance in terms of controlling the escalation of the level of the fighting. This is usually closely related to plans for bringing the war to an end, the 'exit strategy', the actual ending of the war will be considered in a later chapter. The problem of escalation will be considered here.

Once a war has started, even if the causes were trivial and the early engagements on a small scale, there will be a tendency for each of the belligerent governments to steadily increase its fighting forces in its search for a military victory. Unless a natural obstacle puts an end to the fighting then the process of escalation may well continue until one side is

131

obviously out-classed or a state of mutual exhaustion is reached, or the population of one side starts to show a distinct lack of martial enthusiasm. The fighting may well end, but the war cannot be considered really over until the antagonism that caused it has been assuaged. The problem of mutually destructive escalation will be illustrated by a consideration of the Iraq-Iran war of 1980 to 1988.

The two countries have had a record of antagonism reaching back decades, but after the Islamic Revolution of 1979 it reached a new level. The Iranians started to try to extend their position on the Shatt al-Arab and to undermine the Iraqi government urging Shiite Arabs and Kurds to rebel. The upshot was that the Iraqis launched a limited offensive to capture Khorramshahr and occupy the surrounding area on the Shatt al-Arab, but mostly to convince the Iranian government to stop its subversive activities by degrading its armed forces.

The results of the offensive were not as hoped and the Iranian government, which was now under the Ayatollah Khomeini and not very firmly in charge, received a great patriotic boost, the invasion rallying the people behind it. The Iranian forces which, like the Soviets in 1941, had recently had large numbers of their senior officers purged, were either nowhere near the fighting or withdrew very quickly. They were hardly touched.

The Iraqi government under Saddam Hussein made the mistake of limiting the operation, hoping that this would limit the Iranian reaction. They would have done better to have bitten off large areas of Iran to use as bargaining chips later.

The Iranian government, being Islamic fundamentalist, whipped up a great deal of anti-Iraq fervour and pledged to continue the war. At first operations were amateurish and wasteful of life. But, under the necessity of war, they improved and in 1982, while the Iraqis were actually suing for peace, surrounded and destroyed two Iraqi divisions and recaptured Khorramshahr.

The Iraqis then withdrew from Iranian territory and, pointing to the Israeli incursion into the Lebanon, suggested a ceasefire so that troops could be sent to fight them. The Iranians would not listen and insisted in invading Iraq. This turned into a disaster. The Iraqis had increased their forces and dug strong positions behind the border. The Iranians now depended more and more on their Islamic militia, and that depended on militant enthusiasm rather than military skill. The result was human wave assaults even through minefields. Very young volunteers were used for this type of martyrdom. Casualties were heavy but offensive followed offensive with few gains to show for them.

From this point on, despite huge losses little changed. The Iraqis, fearful of an Iranian breakthrough, used mustard and nerve gases, and even electrocuted some Iranians with electrodes fitted in some of the Shatt al-Arab channels. The forces involved increased in size until in some of the later battles some half-a-million troops were deployed.

Slowly, although the Iraqis could not drive the Iranians out of their territory, the balance swung in their favour. They were supplied with arms by many countries, particularly the USSR, the USA and Egypt, which were nervous of an outbreak of Islamic fundamentalism. Conversely Iran's supply of heavy weapons, built up by the Shah, had been largely expended. It is interesting to note that the Iranians were so desperate for spare parts for their tanks that they bought some off Israel! The result of the lack of heavy weapons was that the Islamic militias became more important than the army. This may have contributed to the continuing Iranian faith in fervid human-wave assaults.

As no progress was being made on the ground both sides escalated the scope of the war by bombing, with planes and missiles, each other's cities. The destruction and civilian casualties did not deter the governments from pursuing the war.

A second escalation in scope came when Iraq bombed Iran's oil facilities on Kharg island, and Iran responded by attacking oil tankers bound for Iraq. Iraq responded in kind. This became known as the 'Tanker War', and was to be one of the main causes of the end of the war. The US navy undertook to protect tankers sailing to and from Iraq. The increasing US presence in the Gulf, along with the declining numbers of Iranians volunteering for the front, the destruction of their cities making the functioning of government difficult and the steady improvement of the Iraqi army resulted in the Iranian government calling the war off.

It is difficult to judge the results of this war. It was undertaken to stop Iranian interference in the internal affairs of Iraq and this may well have been achieved, but subsequent events ensured that any success in this direction was short-lived. Either way the results did not in any way justify the sacrifices involved.

The two sides dramatically increased the size of their armed forces throughout the war to a combined total of around 2.5 million. The Iranian reliance on militias makes accurate accounting impossible. It is believed that the war killed around a million people. The economic dislocation and debt caused by the war started a sequence of potentially disastrous events which has not yet been played out.

This war displayed tragically the result of escalation getting out of control. In this case this was based on the types of governments involved. One was a fanatical theocracy and the other a self-centred tyranny. Both showed a contempt for the lives of their troops. This no doubt contributed to the high level of casualties. Even taking that into account this war illustrated very well the perpetual tension between escalation and exit strategy which is a recurring general feature in war, and one which the threat of nuclear weapons will make even more crucial.

The pattern of modern warfare has made negotiations during the war more difficult, even despite the existence of the United Nations. In Napoleonic and earlier times armies were deployed in such a way as to be able to manoeuvre the enemy into accepting a battle, where the fighting was done. The process of manoeuvring was fairly bloodless, in fact the relations between the outposts could even be quite friendly, and governments could talk to each other calmly. In modern wars there are few occasions where battles stand out from manoeuvre in this way, the Falklands war was one. Usually fighting is continuous and the appellation of Battle is given to a period of fighting of greater intensity. This is particularly so in the case of highly mobile operations and reached a high point with the 'Battle of Britain'. Consequently troops must be deployed, and supplied, to be ready for continuous action, and once the war has started governments keep quiet, thus preventing the Clausewitz model working.

As a very brief and over-simplified summary there are two ideal types of deployment of conventional forces. One is based on infantry fighting in which the aim is to destroy the enemy's army. The other is based on tanks and other AFVs and they attempt to achieve their aim by manoeuvring deep in the enemy's territory, surprising and occupying a vital point, and actually fighting as little as possible. In the first case the tanks will be attached to the infantry units, in the second they will be concentrated in armoured divisions. A summary of the British view of warfare is given in Appendix 3.

It may be tempting to assume the AFV based armies are basically offensive in outlook, and infantry based, defensive. But this would be simplistic. All weapons have various characteristics which vary with their presumed deployment. For example the standard infantry rifle will usually be a semi-automatic sighted up to at least 600 yards (metres). This will presume a defensive use. The Russians produce the

AK47, this fired fully automatically but at a shorter range, and was designed for the attack. In fact this type of weapon is known as an Assault Rifle.

This trend shows itself in the design of tanks, the weapons essential to maintaining battlefield mobility in modern warfare. A tank has three main design features: its gun, its armour and its motor. A tank designed for the offensive will be as light as possible, that is with thin armour, so as to be as fast as possible, and with a gun which, if not the most powerful will have a high rate of fire. The defenders will prefer a tank with thick armour, they will tolerate a lower speed, but will want a powerful long-range gun even if it has a low rate of fire.

These trends were displayed during the cold war years in Germany when the Warsaw Pact fielded the T64 and similar tanks, all fast with a low silhouette whereas the British army preferred the Chieftain, a slow moving heavily armoured tank with excellent survivability. The Chieftain was tall compared to the T64 but for the defenders this was not so bad as they could make better use of cover. The Chieftain could depress its gun much more than the T64 which made it easier to take up fire positions on a reverse slope.

The British formations were fully armoured but were designed to fall back in front of a Warsaw Pact advance, delaying it with ambushes and limited counter-attacks.

The tactics for armoured forces in the defence are harder to pin down than those for the attack. The defensive tactics of the NATO forces in West Germany changed steadily throughout the Cold War, but as they were never put to use their effectiveness cannot be properly assessed. In the early days, the 1950s, there was still plenty of infantry, so the general idea was to set up tank-proof areas defended by infantry, with armoured units operating between them putting in counter-attacks as required. The infantry strongpoints would be widely dispersed, sited in depth and well dug in as a precaution against tactical nuclear weapons.

As conscription was abandoned and armies became smaller, infantry became harder to find and tank firepower and general survivability improved, so defence came more to rely on armoured forces. The standard tactic became to fall back in front of the Warsaw Pact troops, setting up ambushes (killing zones), halting the enemy with firepower then counter-attacking.

It was hoped that the greater mobility of these tactics would delay the use of tactical nuclear weapons, or even make their use less likely. The disadvantage was that even a successful counter-attack was unlikely to drive the invaders back across the border. So the attackers, even if halted, would win something.

The final stage of tactical evolution concentrated the tanks into larger units. These were to fall back in front of the attacker while his lengthening supply lines were assaulted by specialised munitions. As the enemy tanks, now being short of fuel, ground to a halt a major counter-attack would start which should destroy the bulk of the enemy tanks, and drive the rest back far over the border. If the war could be halted, or at least the front go firm at this stage, the defenders, NATO, would have gained some territory to bargain with.

The possible use of Battlefield Nuclear Weapons complicates all this. The concentration of troops required for an offensive will offer a very tempting target whereas the defenders will present less of a target if they are scattered along the front in close contact with their enemies. However if the defenders concentrate for a large-scale counter-attack they will become vulnerable in this way. The consequence will be that the first moves in any conflict between first class powers will be to destroy the enemy's surveillance satellites. Uncertainty over the practicability of this should go a long way to deterring the use of even small nuclear weapons.

As can be seen from the above, and as common sense indicates, the defensive is much the stronger form of war. A state with a reasonable army that is not hopelessly outnumbered should be able to sustain a defensive war almost indefinitely. If its forces contain a reasonable number of armoured units they can be deployed to make limited spoiling attacks to disrupt the enemy's offensive preparations. This may be the most efficient use of the defender's troops and was used several times by the Germans on the Eastern front. However a protracted defence may not be a realistic option if there is a need to force the issue. Only an offensive can do that.

At the start of 1918 the German situation was not desperate. The population had endured great shortages, particularly of food, inflicted by the naval blockade, but the recent peace with Russia should have alleviated them. Large numbers of troops were being transferred from the East to the Western front which had stood mostly on the defensive since 1914.

Throughout the war German defensive tactics had steadily improved and had developed into what they termed the 'Elastic Defence'. The principle was that the German front line would be thinly manned. They would fall back in front of an attack, so not to lose men to the artillery barrage. The attackers would then walk into an artillery killing zone, be shot up, then a counter-attack would drive the survivors back to their start line.

Naturally this system did not always work perfectly, but if carried out well it would inflict disproportionately high casualties in return for a minimal loss of ground. Consequently the Germans, having occupied large areas of France and Belgium, had the opportunity of standing on the defensive until the Allies, which now included the USA, after a few costly battles became disillusioned and settled for a negotiated peace.

However the German high command judged that it had to

force the issue and end the war as soon as possible as the German people were starting to show signs of discontent. This was soon after the Russian Revolution, and a wave of strikes, some politically motivated, over the 1917-1918 winter was worrying. Consequently the Germans mounted the Spring offensives which were successful in driving back the British and French armies but did not dent the determination of the Allied governments to pursue the war, and which finally led to the exhaustion of the German army. There is something of a parallel of the Spring offensive with the Ardennes offensive which the Germans mounted in December 1944.

The power of the defensive is why wars, like the Korean War, can end in a stalemate, which is often quite sensible. It may be that many offensives have been mounted at least partly because the commanding generals preferred to be on the offensive, a mode of warfare which is usually regarded as the highest point of their profession.

The 20th century saw a total change in the preparedness of states to build fortifications. The Second World War showed that, with time for planning, the strongest fortifications could be defeated. This was illustrated by the Normandy landings in 1944 and since then by the Egyptian defeat of the Israeli Bar-Lev line on the Suez canal in 1973. By the end of the century the only seriously fortified frontier was the Albanian border with Yugoslavia. This was defended by thousands of shallow-domed concrete pillboxes. These defences can be said to have been effective as no-one has invaded Albania!

If fortifications are now out of favour it is remarkable that few invaded countries have taken any precautions at all. In most cases the reason for this must be that the invasion came as a surprise, but in others perhaps it was judged that preparations would be bad for civilian morale or even some sort of provocation to the potential invader.

In 2003 American and British forces invaded Iraq. This was

not a surprise and the Iraqis had plenty of time to prepare for it. They could have laid mines and carried out demolitions, they could have set up caches of arms, and material for booby-traps close to the few major roads which the invaders would have had to use. In particular they could have hidden anti-aircraft weapons under the flight paths for major airports. By training a small number of men in the use of such weapons they could have inflicted a severe attrition on the invaders, and almost halted the movement of supplies. How effective such a strategy would be can only be gauged by experience, but something can always be done, if only the planning of mass demonstrations and passive resistance. This of course is outside the province of conventional warfare.

In conventional warfare, in particular armoured warfare, the supply situation is of overwhelming importance. It is much easier for the defenders in that supplies can be dumped and the retreating troops fall back to them. Conversely it is much more difficult for the attackers as supplies have to be brought forward often over a devastated landscape and in the face of defensive demolitions. So a study of an army's supply capacity may give a better estimate of its planned deployment than a simple count of its tanks.

Supply difficulties will be greatly increased if the opposing side has command of the air. Tactical air attack of ground targets should be decisive but has in practice usually turned out to be disappointing. However it can be effective against the supply organisation as the aerial bombardment preceding the offensive against the Iraqis in Kuwait in 1991 demonstrated.

Inevitably there is a tendency to use air power instead of ground forces, and this can seem to be an efficient way to bring pressure to bear against a government without enduring the casualties of ground warfare. This may work if that government is unpopular but in reality it has not been that successful. Despite Afghanistan which involved ground forces, the most recent essay at a purely air campaign was the 1999 NATO campaign against Serbia. Its stated aim was to prevent the ethnic cleansing of Kosovar Albanians. It totally failed. It claimed to have destroyed 300 Serb tanks, but the actual number was probably twenty-six AFVs of all kinds. Serbian troops were finally pulled out of Kosovo, but this was not as a result of the air offensive. It was a sensible reaction to Hungary's joining NATO and providing a good quality route which could be used by the NATO Rapid Reaction Corps to invade Serbia if that were felt to be necessary. Further, Serbia's ally, Russia, sent peace-keeping troops to Kosovo to maintain Serbian interests there.

When air power has been used in conjunction with ground forces, as in Iraq in 2003, it has a distinct tendency to be counter-productive. Air Forces have a distaste for operating in direct support of ground troops where they would be little improvement on artillery, but prefer to indulge in 'interdiction'. This is the isolation of the battlefield by destroying roads, bridges, railways and anything else to do with transport. Not only does this fail, but it makes it very difficult for the ground troops to advance after any success they achieve.

The US air offensive against North Vietnam illustrated the difficulty in converting air power into political pressure. In fact clever North Vietnamese propaganda made it something of a negative quantity. The greatest air offensive of all time was mounted against the German and Japanese cities during the Second World War. This was not the original plan for the use of allied bombers, they were expected to be used to destroy enemy industry, but this turned out to be beyond the capacity of the bombers of the period so cities were targeted instead. The logic was that if enough enemy civilians were massacred the enemy would surrender.

The bomber offensive certainly killed hundreds of thousands of German and Japanese civilians and made life very difficult for many more. It also forced the deployment of immense resources in anti-aircraft defence. Conversely, the cost of mounting the bomber offensive was colossal both in industrial and human terms. RAF Bomber Command alone suffered 59,423 killed and missing. These were high quality men who should have been officers and senior ranks in the army. Bomber Command took up industrial production in both heavy industry and technology to a degree that resulted in the army being hampered by poor tanks and a shortage of APCs and radios. Probably worse, a shortage of landing craft was caused which reduced the Allies' strategic options. Considering these facts there is no reason to believe that the conventional bomber offensive against either country shortened the war by even one day. In fact it is possible that the bomber offensive actually prolonged the war, and made post-war reconstruction more difficult. The extent to which the dropping of the Atom Bombs forced the Japanese surrender is still open to question.

The point about post-war reconstruction may carry with it a certain irony in that, to a small extent, the bomber offensive might have been undertaken to downgrade Germany as an industrial nation. The grotesque 'Lindemann Plan', which would have reduced Germany to a sparsely populated pastoral country and permanently changed the European balance of power, is an indication of this. Considerations such as this make a mockery of any claim to morality.

In general air power is best used as an adjunct to ground forces and, if used against the supply system, it should be as close to the battlefield as possible. And this brings consideration back to wars of either attrition based on infantry fighting or mobile operations based on armoured divisions.

In the real world conventional forces and operations fall between these two extremes, but they do illustrate the kind of pressure that conventional warfare can place on governments. In the first case, if its own forces have been destroyed then the government will feel a strong urge to negotiate, observing that the attackers can now do whatever they like. In the second case, the fact of finding the attacker's tanks on their objective will cause deep psychological shock to the population, and such a degree of dislocation of transport and communications that even getting food to the people will become difficult. This will cause civil unrest. Naturally the government will want peace to maintain stability.

The essence of armoured warfare is deep thrusts into the enemy's hinterland, moving so fast that he does not have the opportunity to settle into a defensive position. Naturally this is only possible to achieve against an incompetent, heavily outnumbered or poorly motivated enemy, any other sort will, by demolitions, delaying actions and counter-attacks, be able to force a return to static fighting.

Far ranging deep manoeuvre like this was not possible during the Great War. This was because the attackers could only move slowly through the enemy's lines, but the defenders could rush up reinforcements by rail. The defence was mechanised, the attack was not.

During the 1930s this changed. Good roads, fast tracked AFVs and air support made deep armoured manoeuvre possible, and for this short period up to 1941 and the invasion of Russia, the Germans, under the leadership of Adolf Hitler, were the masters of highly mobile armoured tactics. The Fuhrer was undeniably a genius at this, and it came to be called 'Blitzkrieg', although this term was not used by the German army. His procedure was to weaken the resolve of the victim government by a propaganda offensive, ensure that there would be no foreign intervention, then quickly occupy the target country with airborne and air landing troops, and fast, light armoured columns. Unfortunately, like Napoleon before him and the Israelis after, he failed to convert his stunning and easy victories into a stable and lasting peace.

The implication of all this is that peace negotiations must be carefully calculated and matched to the fighting. If this is not done then the fighting may drag on taking more and more the character of grinding attrition. The great illustration of this comes from the Second World War. The campaign in France in 1940 ended after a general collapse following a German armoured breakthrough. The collapse was as much political as military, and the French signed a treaty which, under the circumstances, was not bad.

Four years later the (jack)boot was on the other foot, but this time the defenders did not collapse and their forces had to be destroyed in heavy infantry based fighting right up to the end. But then, with no army left, the Germans had to accept Unconditional Surrender.

Logistics, the supply of the troops, is the dominant factor in operations. As mentioned above, logistics favour the defence. A retreating army becomes easier to supply as its lines of communication shorten as the attacking army becomes harder to supply. Clausewitz identified what he termed the 'culminating point', when the retreating army, becoming stronger, reached parity with the one advancing. This tendency can be seen in the North African campaigns and in the way the pursuit after Normandy ground to a halt as it approached the German frontier. There is, though, another tendency, and that is for the retreating army to fall apart.

The worst thing for a retreating army is to be fighting on home ground. The very fact of retreat means that discipline is weakening and, as the soldiers are among their own people, the pressure for them to desert, and the opportunity to do so, increases dramatically. This is particularly true when the population can expect to be badly treated by the victors.

Early in 1975 the North Vietnamese Army invaded South Vietnam. The South Vietnamese Army (ARVN) looked impressing on paper and some of its units had fought very well against the North Vietnamese invasion of 1972, but it crumbled. It is true that the North Vietnamese had all the advantages. They had the larger army and held the initiative in that they could, whenever they liked, attack from Laos across a frontier over 500 miles long. Also the South Vietnamese made some very bad operational decisions, but the deciding factor was that the ARVN soldiers deserted in droves. The cause of this was that their families usually lived with them and the triumphant North Vietnamese had a well deserved reputation for massacring their prisoners. Consequently when an ARVN unit received orders to retreat its soldiers were apt to leave their posts to organise their families and to ensure that they were not left behind.

The Vietnamese example was an extreme one but the tendency for units to fall apart will affect any army trying to wage mobile war in its own country.

Urban warfare can be an alternative to mobile warfare. As the world becomes more and more urbanised so the probability of urban warfare increases even though little has been seen of this kind of fighting since 1945. Probably for this reason armies have shown remarkably little interest in preparing for it. In particular no army has developed any AFVs specifically for urban fighting. The full significance of this increasing threat is rather obscure.

The march of technology in general has seen a great increase in the difference in effectiveness between the latest tanks and other machines and the equivalents of them three or four decades earlier. In 2003 in Iraq, T54s were no match for the British Challenger IIs. There can be little doubt that the gap in military effectiveness between first and second rate powers will increase. This difference will be most notable in mobile conventional operations. As operations become static or sub-conventional, so the gap will narrow to some degree.

As has been mentioned under the heading of Sub-Conventional Warfare, in some cases the ethnic situation precludes any reasonable settlement, and large scale population movement has followed. Examples of these include Palestine, India/Pakistan in 1948 and Yugoslavia in the 1990s. The movement of populations should result in their settlement within national borders, but the case of the Palestinians shows that this is not inevitable. The troops, in these circumstances, can do little more than observe the moving crowds and prevent fighting, but this is only a short term fix. Unfortunately the world in general has shown a lamentable lack of sensible long-term planning in this respect.

As can be seen from the above, conventional wars are becoming less and less frequent. This is not to say that it will always be so, but as ethnic boundaries are more in line with national boundaries, and international diplomacy endorses the balance of power, it becomes more difficult to imagine war aims that both government and people would agree on, so the urge to arms will die down. However all nations will retain conventional forces, and occasionally will deploy them to enhance its own prestige. The Indian seizure of Goa was a good example of this, as was the Argentinian invasion of the Falklands

The East Falkland Campaign

Events which caused the Falklands war are a little obscure, but certainly on 15th December 1981 an Argentinian admiral was instructed to prepare a detailed plan for the occupation of the Falklands Islands. From then on it was just a matter of finding a pretext for implementing that plan. When it was found the Falklands were invaded and occupied. The British, rather to the surprise of the Argentinians, sent a task force to retrieve the islands. The basic geography of the theatre of operations meant that the war would be primarily a naval one, but it was inevitable that troops would have to be landed and the Argentinian forces on the main, East Falkland, island would have to be defeated. This is the campaign which will be considered below.

The force sent to the Falklands consisted of two brigades, the 3rd and the 5th. The bulk of the 3rd Brigade landed on the night of $21^{st}/22^{nd}$ May 1982 at San Carlos Bay during and after an epic battle in which the British war ships came under sustained attack from Argentinian planes. The cargo and troops carrying ships were located so that to a degree they were sheltered by high ground, but even so the Argentinian decision not to concentrate on them is puzzling and a huge piece of luck for the British.

Special forces were helicoptered in to secure the beaches and neutralise an Argentinian position on Fanning Head, the point of the peninsula covering the entrance to San Carlos Bay. In the first wave of landing craft were eight light tanks, Scorpions and Scimitars, which took up positions to secure the beaches from counter-attack. Four battalion sized units were landed on the first night, soon to be followed by a fifth. As soon as it was ashore one battalion (2nd Battalion, the Parachute Regiment), still dripping wet, marched off southwards to occupy Mt Sussex to defend against a possible counter-attack from the Darwin isthmus.

Once the brigade was ashore the problem facing it looked simple enough, it was to capture the town of Stanley, approximately fifty miles away. The main part of the East Falkland island is of a very irregular but roughly circular shape. To the south-west there is a sizeable extension called Lafonia connected to the mainland by the Darwin isthmus. The terrain is bleak moorland and low, craggy mountains. Stanley stands on a peninsula on the eastern side of the island, opposite to San Carlos. The Argentinians had set up three lines of defence, based on high ground, running across this peninsula, the outermost being twelve miles from Stanley.

One of the remarkable aspects of the Falklands War was that control of the British Task Force, both naval and military, was retained by the Task Force commander, Admiral Sir

John Fielding, from his HQ at Northwood, England, and not delegated to an officer with the Task Force. Soon after the landing the brigade commander received an order from Northwood to, initially, raid the Goose Green settlement of the Darwin isthmus, then it was altered to an order to capture it. This order precipitated the Battle of Goose Green, which has become the most studied battalion scale battle the world has seen. It was not an order welcomed by the brigade which had quite enough to do planning the move on Stanley, but it was judged necessary to get the land campaign started, with a victory, before international pressure for a ceasefire became irresistible.

The obvious unit to send to Goose Green was the 2nd Bn, the Parachute Regiment which, having been posted at Mt Sussex, was the closest. The Brigade Commander could offer the battalion little support, little more than three 105mm howitzers. Some of the CVRs would have made a huge difference, but it was feared that they would bog down in the soft peat and not be available for the decisive drive on Stanley. Due to a shortage of helicopters the battalion had to march to its start line, about 15 miles. The shortage of transport meant minimal ammunition for the guns and mortars, insufficient batteries for the radios, and few creature comforts, like sleeping bags, for the soldiers in very bleak weather conditions.

The Colonel's battle plan has been the subject of endless controversy. Essentially it was to attack at night, 27th/28th May, proceeding on a series of phase lines. The companies were to be widely spaced and had, in some cases five miles, as the crow flies, to cover. For night fighting tight control is necessary to prevent 'blue on blue' encounters, and because of the difficulty in providing artillery support, which at Goose Green would come from HMS Arrow.

The weakness of the plan was that the whole operation was too ambitious to be concluded in one night. In the morning HMS Arrow sailed away and, with failing batteries, intercompany communications became difficult. The situation was not helped by the Colonel insisting on being in the front line where, almost inevitably, he was killed.

The Argentinian defence was static and in each action the British proved themselves the better soldiers and steadily gained ground. After the Colonel's death the companies on the western flank, now permitted to move independently, continued slowly, in the face of heavy fire, to move round to envelope Goose Green. The Argentinian commander must have assumed a relentless British plan and next morning when he was requested to surrender, he did.

The Colonel's actions in the battle are usually criticised, but were entirely logical from his point of view. He knew that his battalion had a large task in front of it and the battle had to be won at night, daylight would, and did, slow everything down. He believed that the Argentinians would 'fold' if hit hard enough, so the only hope was in aggression, so he was in the front line to urge his company commanders on. Unfortunately plans which require the enemy not to fight can easily become unstuck as an earlier generation of the same regiment found at Arnhem.

However the Colonel's heroics were not in vain. When the Argentinians, both officers and other ranks, heard of the death of a British Colonel leading an infantry charge, they knew they would lose.

The battle of Goose Green illustrates the two different command styles. These are usually called 'directive control' and 'restrictive control'. In the first the subordinate commanders are told what their objectives and time frame are and left to get on with it. In the second they are rigidly controlled and in an attack, as at Goose Green, they proceed via phase lines. Naturally restrictive control is necessary when the troops are attacking behind a creeping barrage or when communications with the artillery are difficult. Conversely in mobile fighting directive control must be used or the initiative might be lost. These two styles of leadership, in the context of Goose Green, will be discussed for years to come.

Just before and during the Goose Green battle events crowded in. A cargo ship, the Atlantic Conveyor, was sunk. All but one of the helicopters aboard which had been so eagerly awaited were lost. Fortunately this disaster was to be balanced by the destruction of most of the Argentinian helicopters by British planes, so if British mobility was hampered, so was the Argentinian.

The highest mountain in the outer defence line of Stanley is Mt Kent. The Argentinian unit stationed there was moved to try, but failed, to intervene in the Goose Green battle. Its absence was noted by a special forces patrol and, after some hair-raising sparring between opposing special forces, Mt Kent was occupied by elements of a Royal Marine commando flown in by helicopter. Two other battalion sized units were already on their way, by foot, initially to Teal Inlet where the fleet would come as soon as possible, then on to the battles round Stanley.

If the Colonel's actions at Goose Green had surprised the Argentine command, the ability of British helicopter pilots to fly in the terrible weather and the marching speed of the British soldiers and marines were even more unwelcome surprises. In fact the impression of the campaign is that at this stage the war was being won by 3rd Brigade and available shipping should have been dedicated to its logistic support.

While the Mt Kent operation was proceeding, the 5th Brigade started to arrive at San Carlos. It seems that the original idea was that this unit would provide garrisons and security to allow 3rd Brigade to get on with the war, but this was changed when the new divisional commander took over. He decided to attack Stanley with two brigades, the 3rd to the north. The troops marched and the Navy supplied them via

Teal Inlet. The 5th Brigade went to the south.

This decision caused the greatest disaster of the war. Two Guards battalions were to move to Fitzroy. They tried to march but the going was found to be too soft so the Navy was called on to transport them. Half of one battalion was caught aboard ship by some Argentinian planes and suffered very heavy casualties, including 39 deaths, effectively destroying two companies. Shortly before this a Royal Navy ship had, through no fault of its own, shot down an army helicopter, killing the four men in it. These events point to a lack of coordination between the amphibious force, naval warships and the army. This may have been a result of too much control being retained by Northwood, a lack of understanding of the requirements of amphibious warfare at divisional level or irresponsible behaviour at a lower level.

A further major problem was that 5th Brigade arrived without any transport. Naturally this caused a hold up in the logistics build up to the climactic battles of the campaign.

The outer line of the Argentinian defences of Stanley was dominated by Mt Kent which had already fallen to the British, and the whole line was abandoned. Probably it was never planed to make a protracted defence on this line as it was almost beyond the range of the artillery based at Stanley. The Argentinians deployed 105mm and 155mm guns, fortunately they only had a small number of the latter. The 155s could just support Mt Kent, the 105s could not.

The main line of defence depended on three mountains, though the expression 'mountains' is something of an overstatement. They were, from the north, Mt Longdon, Two Sisters and Mt Harriet. Longdon peaked at 600', Two Sisters at 1000 and Harriet at 900. The Argentinians had laid extensive minefields but had not put up any barbed wire, an amazing omission. Even if the Royal Navy had prevented bringing some from Argentina there must have been plenty available locally had the military authorities looked for it. It might not have had military barbs but it would have been good enough.

The line was assaulted and captured on the night of 11th/12th June by the 3rd Brigade. Each of the main positions was attacked by a battalion sized unit, Longdon by a Parachute battalion, the others by Royal Marine Commandos. The assaults were timed so that each would facilitate the next, though in the event this sequence broke down with no obviously bad results. The three battles were close enough together that fire support from the 105mm batteries could be switched from one to the other quite easily, and naval gunfire was particularly effective. In the open moorland the peat could deaden explosions, but the rocky mountain tops could not, in fact by producing rock fragments they made the artillery more effective.

Although there were plans for exploitation, the intensity of the fighting was such that the troops were glad to 'go firm' on their objectives.

As soon as possible after the 3rd Brigade assault the inner defences were attacked, this was on the night of 13th/14th June. 3rd Brigade's reserve battalion went through to capture Wireless Ridge. This battalion, 2nd Bn, the Parachute Regiment, was the only one to fight two battles in this campaign. This battle was notable for the deployment of two CVR light tanks, where their sophisticated night sights were found to be very useful.

On the south of the line, 5th Brigade, consisting of two battalions, Guards and Gurkhas, attacked firstly Mt Tumbledown, with the Guards, then the Gurkhas went on to Mt William which they found to be abandoned by its defenders. Despite the fact that these were the last battles of the campaign they were very hard fought, Tumbledown alone resulted in nine British dead and 43 wounded. The last feasible Argentine defensive position was on Sapper Hill, but the campaign was obviously lost, everyone realised it and the fighting just ground to a halt.

These comments conclude this brief summary of the campaign. Various aspects of it will now be considered.

There can be little doubt that the war would not have been fought at all if the British government had made it plain that it could, and would, fight. This represented a total failure of deterrence, brought about by letting negotiations drag on.

The news broadcasts of the BBC were very informative, even to the extent of telling the world that a Parachute battalion was poised to assault Goose Green the next day, and a few days later that the 3rd Brigade supply base had been moved to Teal Inlet. Fortunately the Argentinians chose not to believe that this information could possibly be true, as no responsible organisation would broadcast it if it were. They did, though, take notice when the BBC told the world that their bombs were not fused properly for low level attacks on ships.

Once the Argentinians realised that the British would fight their strategy was sensible. They would dig in and hold out until the winter, shortage of supplies and world opinion forced the British to admit defeat. This strategy only failed because of the amazing ability of the Royal Navy to put together a task force containing many merchant ships so quickly at such short notice.

The war itself could reasonably be called the 'Last of the Gentlemen's Wars', an epithet previously used to describe the Boer War. The British could have taken the mountain positions easily by napalming them, but sportingly preferred to lose men fighting for them in the old fashioned way. This decision may well have been justifiable in terms of gaining, and retaining, international opinion and support, and not horrifying British voters, but if the assaults had failed a different view may have been taken. The war cost 253 British lives, a small number being merchant seamen employed by the Royal Navy. Three Falkland Islanders were killed by 'friendly fire'.

Likewise the Argentines surrendered rather than see Stanley, and the people in it, flattened. No doubt this was sensible militarily, the campaign was lost, but a reluctance to attract international odium must have played a part.

Running the war from Northwood was not a success, but as communications improve there can be little doubt that the trend will be to exert this kind of long range control. It will always be the case that for operational decisions there is just no substitute for the human contact of a traditional 'O' group.

On the purely tactical level there was a surprisingly large number of failings and shortages on the British side. As the Soviet Marshal Chuikov commented, *"in war, as a rule, there is a shortage of something or another"*, but these failings were hidden by the quality of the officers and men and their ability to muddle through.

There was too little use made of the Scorpion and Scimitar light tanks (CVR(T) - Combat Vehicles Reconnaissance, Tracked). Only eight, and a recovery vehicle, were sent to the Falklands. This was a pity. The ability to cross very soft ground was a basic design specification for these vehicles. They are light, in fact one can be stood on four one-pint beer glasses. They have many variants including a personnel carrier, and can be carried by Chinook helicopters. The Soviets had shown during the Ogaden war, when they helicoptered in troops in AFVs to bypass the heavily defended Kara Marda pass, that this kind of mobility is feasible and a potential battle winner. As the Wireless Ridge battle showed they have an excellent night fighting capability. If all this had been taken into account when the task force was being set up and more CVRs sent then the fighting, particularly at Goose Green, would have been over much more quickly and at less cost.

Finally there was the basic quality of the troops. Not only were the British troops regulars but training areas in Britain tend to be bleak moorlands. This had the effect of making the training seem relevant and was confidence enhancing. The opposite was true for the Argentinians. They were conscripts, their best troops were retained in the Argentine to watch Chile. They had little training and what they had was based on internal security operations. The bleak moorland was alien to them. They could stand in a trench and fire machine guns as bravely as anyone, but when called on to manoeuvre they

were outclassed. It was no shame for them to be beaten by the British army.

A glance at the naval side of the campaign underlines a point made in Chapter 2 about how specialising in one type of warfare can reduce effectiveness in others. In the years before the Falklands campaign the Royal Navy had run down its amphibious capacity to specialise in anti-submarine operations and its ships were designed accordingly. Unfortunately this made them less able to defend themselves against, and survive, attacks by planes, than the ships of the Second World War were. Hopefully this has been corrected in the next generation of warships.

As the economic balance of the world changes and China and India become industrial super-powers, inevitably British interests will dictate a more amphibious strategy and the British army will return to its traditional role of a projectile fired by the Navy. The expertise gained in the Falklands War should assist this.

7

Regime Change

Insurrection or Intervention?

The previous two chapters have discussed the practical aspects of horizontal and vertical warfare. Occasionally there are circumstances when a deliberate choice may be made as to which of the two forms of war should be used. Most commonly this is when one country wants to see a regime change in another. The two methods are either to invade the country, change the government and leave, a process often termed 'military intervention', or to foment an internal insurrection and leave the regime change to the rebels.

Naturally the best and most efficient use of the insurrection method would be to sponsor a *coup d'état*. Providing the new government seems patriotic and not obviously the creature of its sponsors it may be accepted by the people and the war aim will have been achieved with minimal cost. Remarkably when the US and Great Britain invaded Iraq in 2003 planning for a coup to oust Saddam Hussein was in an advanced stage. Had this coup been supported instead of the invasion then thousands of lives and billions of dollars might have been saved.

Usually there is no real choice of method. In 1944 it was out of the question for the Allies to wait for some nebulous German anti-Nazi resistance to bring Hitler down, their policy of demanding Unconditional Surrender had effectively ruled that out so a conventional campaign was obviously necessary. Similarly the US could hardly invade Afghanistan in the 1980s, but could assist the anti-Soviet insurrection covertly. There will be times, though, when there will be a real choice and when this happens the second of these options, the internal insurrection, would seem to be the obviously preferable one if at all possible but, as has been shown, it is only very seldomly attempted.

There are several reasons for this. Fomenting an internal insurrection can take a long time, it can be practically difficult, it involves a potential loss of power in that the new government could be difficult, and it is unpredictable.

The factor of time is important in foreign wars, long running conflicts always become unpopular whereas a short, fast campaign gives the leaders an aura of competence and efficiency. The practical difficulties are easier to overcome if the instigating and victim countries share a common border, as was the case with North and South Vietnam, but this is not an absolute necessity as the US showed in Afghanistan. The Afghan example illustrates the third and fourth problems, the loss of the political power over the forces involved. In this case, not too many years passed before the US was fighting against the same Afghans it had previously armed as anti-communist heroes.

As a rule, providing it is at all possible the invasion option will be chosen. This will be so for the converse of the reasons for insurrection. The aggressor can strike quickly. Having the training, planning and equipment the task should not be that difficult. He stays in full control and everything should run according to plan. There is also a fifth reason. Nurturing an insurrectionary movement is a long and subtle process and, as Tacitus wrote around nineteen centuries ago *"most people consider the military mind is lacking in subtlety"*. Soldiers will naturally tend to recommend the invasion option.

It must not be forgotten that, however much the North Vietnamese sponsored the Viet Cong, in the end they mounted a conventional invasion of the South which they have dominated ever since. This, of course, was a simple war of conquest, but the operational choices were the same as for a regime change.

The great disadvantage of the invasion method is that the

new government will inevitably be seen by the population as being merely the creature of the invaders, as the British found in two Afghan wars in the nineteenth century. If the new government needs supporting, as it is likely to, then the invasion will turn into an occupation, and this will evoke resistance from many patriotic elements so an asymmetric warfare situation may develop which will be discussed in the next chapter. The best scenario is when an invasion, or even better the threat of one, triggers a regime change. This is what happened in Guatemala in 1954 when an invasion force of 150 poorly trained and led rebels, aided by very clever CIA propaganda, induced President Arbenz to resign. It may be that the easy success of this operation resulted in the CIA being a little over-confident when planning its next attempted regime change operation.

This next operation, which resulted in the Bay of Pigs disaster, was to provide a good example of the insurrection/invasion choice, and the mistakes that can be made.

Following the success of the Communist revolution in Cuba, in 1959, a large number of Cuban exiles took up residence in Florida. They soon started making plans for their return to Cuba, but to do this they had to topple the Castro government. The USA also wanted to see Castro removed, so naturally the Cubans were armed and encouraged by the US government via the CIA.

A number of the exiles, some of whom had actually fought alongside Castro, advocated a '*foco*' type strategy. Guerrilla bases would be set up in mountainous areas, and the guerrillas supplied by the US by air. How successful this would have been is impossible to gauge. The great weakness was political. The exiles were of every political hue, some being disillusioned Communists, some were supporters of the Batista regime that Castro replaced, and others were moderate politicians unhappy with the anti-democratic nature of Castro's government. Not surprisingly they could not agree on a unifying political agenda. The result was that the Cuban people would inevitably regard them as counter-revolutionary. It is true that Castro's government was not absolutely popular, but it was making progress with land reform, and was much more popular than the government it had overthrown, so no-one wanted a return to that. Consequently the Cuban government was not vulnerable in the way the Guatemalan one was.

Furthermore its security forces were improving. The Batista army had been disbanded and a new one, of roughly 30,000 men, recruited. It seems that Castro was not entirely sure of its loyalty. To back it up and to provide a counter-balance he set up a Revolutionary Militia of between 200,000 and 300,000 men though they were not all armed and many had negligible military training. Also he set up a political police service to keep an eye on potential rebels.

The exiles' lack of a party line was worrying. A guerrilla movement will not be successful if it is run on liberal-democratic lines. The dangers and hardships involved require ruthless discipline, and its policies must be simple, unambiguous and unquestioningly supported by the guerrillas. These policies must also appeal to the country people. The exiles could not manage this. Unfortunately they did not have the time to work on it as it was ascertained that the Cuban air force was soon to be supplied with Czechoslovakian fighters, and for that reason it was judged that if any action was to be taken, it had better be soon.

Mostly for the sake of getting on with the job it was decided to launch a conventional invasion. There were several problems with this. Most importantly the USA was not popular within Cuba. The Cubans believed, with some justification, that they had been exploited by American business, particularly sugar companies, and if the invasion were seen to be just a cover for US imperialism they would have closed ranks against it. However without US military hardware and expertise such a difficult operation could hardly have taken place.

The compromise arrived at resulted in the invasion force being small and, because of the US not wanting to be seen to be involved, behaving hesitantly. The military component was a paratroop unit, three infantry battalions, and one each of armour and artillery. The armoured battalion actually consisted of five light tanks and a few wheeled vehicles armed with machine guns. The force was to be transported in five landing craft and six small freighters, all of which were Cuban exile manned. The invaders were given a small air force of twenty B26 light bombers.

In its initial form the plan might, just, have worked. It involved setting up a propaganda broadcasting station then inserting small teams to co-ordinate resistance. Air attacks would destroy the Cuban air force on the ground and write down their armoured forces. The invaders would land close to mountainous terrain so as to be able to quickly set up a secure base area and they would take with the a large number of small arms with which to arm the numerous recruits who would flock in. Support for the Castro government would crumble.

Alas, in the event all this turned out to be wishful thinking.

The propaganda broadcasts seem to have had no effect on the peasants and, as soon as the air raids started the newly set up political police rounded up anyone who could feasibly be regarded as a threat to the regime. Around a quarter of a million people were arrested. This ensured that there would be no public sympathy for the invaders.

The B26 bombing raids failed to destroy the Cuban air force. The bulk of the Cuban planes were inoperable anyway so any figure of planes destroyed will be a little vague. Certainly two armed jet trainers and two Hawker Sea Fury fighters of WWII vintage survived. The first raid was fairly successful but the second was cancelled by order of

President Kennedy, a decision which is still controversial. Then the landing forces went in.

The initial plan was to land at Trinidad, but this area is heavily populated, and it is believed that because of fear of civilian casualties the President insisted on a change to the *Bahia de Cochinos*. This translates, rather unfortunately, as 'The Bay of Pigs', though in Cuba *'cochinos'* can also mean a type of fish. The new site was handy for an air strip which was long enough for B26s to use, but it was away from the sanctuary of the mountains and easily cut off as the terrain inland from the beaches was swampy.

The actual landings went almost as well as could be hoped, in view of the difficulty of the task and the low level of training of the troops. The paratroops were dropped at two locations. At one they were quickly captured by militia, but at the other they occupied an important cross-roads ten miles inland. The plan was to land on three beaches, one battalion on each. Because of loss of surprise one landing was cancelled and the battalion involved was transferred to another beach. On one of the beaches a battalion landed with some tanks and started its move inland, but on the other, due to shallow water and coral reefs that the aluminium and fibre-glass boats could not cross, and probably a lack of initiative and drive in the command structure, one battalion did not land. The one that did got so wet that its radios would not work.

The landings were carried out at night. The idea being by dawn to have the ships far out to sea where the Cuban planes could not reach them. This was too optimistic a plan for such a force. In the morning, 17th April 1961, the ships and landing craft were still close to shore and the Cuban planes attacked, sinking one and driving the rest away. The troops ashore were now understrength, without most of their vehicles and reserve ammunition, and almost *incommunicado*.

The Cuban forces acted commendably quickly. They initially suffered one or two setbacks, local militia units being defeated and an advancing column being hit by B26s, but soon the Cuban planes, having seen off the ships, shot some B26s down and drove the rest from the skies. The Cuban forces closed in, and, cut off from resupply and pounded by artillery and aircraft, the invaders surrendered on 19th April. Of the 1,189 men who surrendered the vast majority were released after two years in exchange for $53,000,000's worth of aid.

The Bay of Pigs operation is so surrounded by propaganda and opinion that it is hard to be objective about it. But it must be that the critical factor was the loyalty and activity of the Cuban militia. If these units had joined the invaders, or even just refused to fight, the invasion might just have been successful. The failure to suborn these units, or their leaders, resulted in Castro staying in power a further 47 years.

It was stated earlier that an invasion, providing the forces involved had the training, planning and equipment, should not be that difficult. The Bay of Pigs disaster shows what can happen if these conditions have not been met.

There has been a large number of successful regime change operations since 1945, mostly via sponsored coups. It is remarkable that in only very few cases have these operations improved the lot of the people of the countries involved. One that was a success in this direction was the British-backed coup in the Oman in 1970. Unfortunately the greater number has resulted in worse regimes, for instance Idi Amin (British sponsored) in Uganda, and General Pinochet (US sponsored) in Chile. The reasons for this trend are obscure.

It is likely that as the process of globalisation proceeds the stresses caused will evoke many more regime change operations. Judging by the past this will not be a good thing.

162

8

Asymmetric Warfare

This form of warfare has been touched upon several times already. This section will bring all of these strands together. Asymmetric warfare usually sees the government of a highly sophisticated country in conflict with the people of a relatively unsophisticated one. One variation may be a super-national government in conflict with one of its less sophisticated nations. There may be other variations but the essential point is the difference in the level of sophistication and development of the armed forces and, usually, the social systems of the belligerents.

The term 'asymmetric warfare' is an imprecise one and it may be doubted how necessary or useful it is. But as the term is in common use by the news media, this chapter is necessary.

This kind of warfare was common in the 19th Century when the European empires were expanding. Their modern armies were usually pitted against uncivilised tribesmen. However with the march of civilisation there are no longer uncivilised countries but asymmetric warfare has continued, at least partly because some relatively unsophisticated countries are no longer satisfied with their place in the world and seek to change it, resulting in military intervention by those threatened by this change. In the modern world asymmetric warfare often involves low levels of hostility across an international border. This scenario describes the current Arab/Israeli situation.

In an ideal asymmetric case the more sophisticated power invades and defeats the armed forces of the defending government in a one-sided conventional campaign. This is a standard example of horizontal (national) warfare. This stage will probably be followed by a period of sub-conventional warfare when the remains of the defeated army and civilian resistance fight against the occupying troops and among themselves. This is an example of vertical warfare. The conventional campaign will have resulted in the erosion, or destruction, of the prestige of the defeated government, and this will result in an outbreak of anarchy. The victors will find that either they have no defeated government to negotiate with, or that the government is powerless to enforce its orders on the people. The victors find that they have to stay and maintain order even if only to create a government that will admit defeat.

The invader's response to the vertical phase will be hampered by its command and force structures being organised for conventional warfare, and it will take some time to reorganise and retrain for security operations, as Coalition forces found after the 2003 invasion of Iraq.

If the occupiers are successful the war will fade away, resistance will cease and the occupiers will leave, leaving behind a government that they approve of and a social system acceptable to the local population. If the resisters are successful they will inflict a rate of attrition on the occupiers too great for the government to sustain in that it will usually evoke an anti-government outcry which, sooner or later, must be heeded. The upshot is that the occupiers will leave, leaving behind a government they do not approve of and a lasting degree of bitterness.

In fact most asymmetric wars start as being raids into the country in order to change a regime, burn a few crops or take any other action that would relieve the situation. Then the attacking force gets bogged down in fighting and has to be reinforced. This mobilises opinion against the invaders which, in turn, escalates the fighting.

This kind of raid has very seldom been a success, and its most recent (at the time of writing) failure was demonstrated by the Israelis in July 2006 by their incursion into the Lebanon. The virulently anti-Jewish militants of Hezbollah had become established close to the border with Israel and started bombarding Israeli towns and settlements with rockets. Then on 12th July a raid captured two Israeli soldiers. Soon afterwards Israeli armoured columns pounded into Lebanon intent on destroying Hezbollah. Initially world opinion was generally favourable, and even some Arab countries, suspicious of Iranian aims, they being the backers of Hezbollah, were not anti-Israel.

However the armoured columns did not achieve their aim. Hezbollah was not destroyed. Casualties mounted, the Israeli tanks, the much-touted Merkavas, proved embarrassingly vulnerable, the rockets kept coming, vast numbers of houses were destroyed, and a large number of Arab children and other non-combatants were killed. World opinion turned against the Israelis and after around three weeks their forces were withdrawn. It would not be true to say that the Israelis had been directly defeated by Hezbollah, but the fact is that they were not in a position to undertake the sustained operations that destroying Hezbollah would require. Any failure to achieve the war aims is a defeat, and the Israelis failed.

This Israeli defeat gave an immense boost to the Arab world, particularly Iran. Amazingly the Israelis undertook a measure to ensure lasting enmity. In the last two or three days of the campaign, in fact after the United Nations resolution demanding their withdrawal had been passed, they scattered thousands of bomblets in the areas where Hezbollah had been operating. These bomblets explode only when disturbed, so the price would be paid by Lebanese farmers and their children for years to come.

On 16th July 2008 the remains of the two soldiers were returned to Israel in exchange for five prisoners and the remains of 199 others.

One very depressing aspect of this operation was the total lack of any sensible judgement of what can be achieved by conventional warfare. This is one of the recurring themes of history.

Sensible judgements are harder to make when there is an extra-national organisation ensconced in one country which takes military action against another, which was the case in the example cited above. The government of the injured nation will look to the government of the host nation to extradite the perpetrators or pay reparations. Ultimately, if it cannot get satisfaction, it may invade, as the US did in Afghanistan in 2001. In this case the Taliban regime had provided sanctuary and support for Al Qaeda. The regime was soon overthrown and replaced by one acceptable to the west, but Al Qaeda remained and soon large numbers of US, British and other nations' troops were committed to fighting them, and, at least in theory, assisting the Afghan government in doing that.

However, local loyalties being what they are in underdeveloped countries, it can be seen that Robespierre's dictum (quoted in Chapter 10) about invaders being repelled as enemies would soon apply. At the time of writing these operations are still in train.

Invading a country under these conditions is quite reasonable in terms of international law as when a nation cannot prevent organisations within its borders from launching military operations then it has lost the right to be regarded as an independent nation. But in practice this kind of operation is seldom a success.

It can happen that the government of the unsophisticated country invites in troops from a sophisticated one in order to take advantage of their high-tech weaponry and high level of training. Such a case is illustrated by the Ethiopians and the Ogaden War. In 1977 Somalia, which had been supplied with weapons by the USSR, decided to send home their Soviet advisers and invade Ogaden, a Somali speaking province of Ethiopia. The Soviets then stopped supplying Somalia and suggested an alliance with Ethiopia. This worked out well for both parties. Ethiopia wanted Ogaden back, and the USSR wanted to extend its influence in Africa, as it was doing apparently successfully in Angola.

The result of this alliance was a large quantity of weapons which included an armoured task force. Some Soviet technicians were supplied to maintain the high-tech weapons, but the bulk of the AFV crews were Cuban. There were around 11,000 Cubans. There was also a South Yemeni contingent, but these soldiers do not seem to have distinguished themselves.

This armoured task force, ably supported by war planes, paratroops and armoured vehicle carrying helicopters, reconquered Ogaden in an impressive and fast campaign. But with that, conventional warfare had reached its limit. Ethiopia was a highly unstable country suffering from several insurgent movements and constant fighting, most notably in Eritrea. Even worse, a number of senior officers were purged following an abortive *putsch*. These considerations, and the internal situation of the USSR, resulted in the USSR withdrawing its financial support, and the last of the Soviet and Cuban soldiers were withdrawn in 1989.

Despite the high degree of skill shown during the Soviet campaign, putting armoured columns in the middle of a third world country does not automatically make that country a useful ally.

Asymmetric warfare can be the result of a mixture of conventional and sub-conventional operations being carried out in the same war. The 'Amritsar Massacre' has been described in an earlier chapter. This incident should be seen in the context of the Third Afghan War. It restored order in the Punjab and allowed troops to be moved to confront the Afghans and bring operations against them to a successful conclusion. Without 'Amritsar' the war would have dragged on and the casualties could have been much heavier. Chapter 12 shows how bad the results of anarchy in a place like the Punjab could be.

The Americans in Vietnam faced a similar problem. They had to fight against large units of the North Vietnamese Army in conventional-type operations. This was what General Westmoreland referred to as the 'big unit war'. At the same time they had to be fighting, and assisting the South Vietnamese forces fighting, the Viet Cong guerrillas. This resulted in many pictures of the US soldiers with tanks, helicopters and the full panoply of conventional war in action against pitiful village guerrillas. Pictures that were so useful to communist propaganda. The war is remembered as a guerrilla war, but the big units won it, and those units were North Vietnamese.

When large conventional units of the sophisticated power are challenged by the conventional forces of the unsophisticated power the sophisticates usually win, and, as campaigns in Iraq have shown, win easily. This, though, is not inevitable, and there have been cases when the more basic army fighting in terrain which has suited its methods, has routed its opponents. The best example of this is the rout of the UN troops at the Battle of the Chongchon River, in 1950, when the Chinese first entered the Korean War. The Chinese, having few vehicles, were not dependent on roads to the expected extent and also they usually moved only at night, so aerial reconnaissance which had proven so useful in Europe was rendered almost blind. The countryside being fought over, consisting of many steep-sided ridges and hills, reduced the effectiveness of the UN artillery and made this artillery difficult to manoeuvre. Consequently the Chinese 'circle and block' tactics worked very well, and UN troops that found Chinese behind them threatening their supply lines had to fall back making themselves vulnerable to ambushes. If the Chinese could be forced to stand and fight, then because they carried little in the way of ammunition and other supplies with them, they soon had to break off the action, but it was some time before this was realised. There are parallels here with the experiences of the British forces facing the Japanese during the early Japanese offensives.

The most pressing problem with asymmetric warfare has always been how to bring it to a satisfactory and stable conclusion, and the measures taken have changed over the years. During the expansion of the empires these wars were caused by uncivilised tribes outside the imperial borders raiding across them. To put a stop to this the locals would demand a war though, because of the expense, this was seldom popular with the government of the colonial power. But once the army had occupied the tribal territory it found that the easiest way to achieve a lasting peace was for the colonial government to incorporate that territory into its empire. The French empire spread across vast tracts of Africa in the face of lack of imperial enthusiasm from Paris because of pressure from the local administrators. The French army even lied to Paris about the location of its troops to keep up the march of empire.

The British experience was similar, except for the lies. The advantage of incorporating the invaded country in the empire was that the new administration was going to be permanent, consequently a degree of loyalty would develop towards it. If, on the other hand, the invaders would soon be leaving, the people must always look for accommodation with the ruthless forces that would come out on top later.

This model has its variants. For example in what was to become Southern Rhodesia the Mashonas wanted to be taken under British rule, which was at the time in the form of a chartered company, as a protection against Matabele raids. This was initially a success, but soon they found that the organisation, and taxes, of civilisation were not to their liking, and revolted. As by the time of the revolt there had been considerable British immigration into Mashonaland, it could not be allowed to succeed, and the Mashonas stayed in the Empire.

On two occasions in the 19th Century the British in India, who had constant friction with Afghanistan, tried to achieve a settlement by invading that country and setting up a friendly ruler. In both occasions it was easy to install the ruler, but soon resistance built up against him, not surprisingly as any ruler set up by non-Muslims would not be popular with the Afghans. The result in both cases was heavy fighting and many British and Indian casualties. This is probably what Olaf Caroe, who was the penultimate British Governor of the North-West Frontier Province, meant when he wrote, "*unlike other wars, Afghan wars become serious only when they are over*". Ultimately it was accepted that Afghanistan and the British Empire had to be separated by an area where lawlessness and constant skirmishing prevailed.

The great complication of asymmetric warfare is the difference in levels of civilisation of the protagonists. The less sophisticated country, the one usually occupied by the troops of the other, will have a weak central government so it will tend to consist of what amounts to the personal fiefs of local warlords, to use a common and appropriate newspaper term. These warlords do not rise to prominence through hard work or commerce but, ultimately, through the skill-at-arms of their supporters. Consequently, although they cannot match the occupying forces in large scale conventional warfare, they will have far more experience of small scale operations, as the Russians found in Afghanistan, and the Americans found in Somalia.

Assuming the intervention has not been a great success the occupying power will have to make a tricky decision about when to leave. One option, and the one that always seems best in retrospect, is to leave as soon as possible, secure in the knowledge that the occupied country has been brought to a degree of chaos and is unlikely to be a threat to anyone for a number of years. Unfortunately leaving under these circumstances involves admitting defeat, or at least admitting having made a mistake, so political pressure will try to prevent it. Also there might be important practical reasons, for example oil, for leaving a friendly, stable government in power. This situation can show the recurring problem with asymmetric warfare already referred to. The initial phase has been carried out under military leadership, but the second requires political control. The switch is seldomly achieved in a timely and sensible way, and too much military control can be inimical to the political phase.

Usually maintaining public order, and keeping potential insurgents under control, will be the immediate priority for the departing power. In the early two-thousands-and-teens this was done along the Afghanistan/Pakistan border by remotely controlled drones. These killed many people, and no doubt some of these were insurgents, but it is impossible to imagine a system further away from the 'bobby on the beat' model. Inevitably the peace upheld by such means was to crumble as soon as they were withdrawn.

The problem for the departing power may come down to finding a potential government to deal with and that government must be regarded as legitimate by the people. In this context it was a disaster, in 2003, when the invaders disbanded and dispersed the Iraqi army, which should have been used as a prop for the government giving it that degree of legitimacy. It will be found that just backing the local strongman will not work as, to establish his nationalistic credentials, he will be antagonistic to the occupiers. However a government based on local grandees will try to maintain civil order and this will be of great advantage to the occupiers. Failing this the occupiers will face the task of improving the level of civilisation of the occupied country to the point when the new government will be able to function and will be acceptable. Every military action they undertake should be done with this in mind, regardless of tactical considerations. There are depressingly few cases this ever being achieved. One case such was the US occupation of the Philippines during the early part of the 20th Century.

Without any improvement in the level of civilisation, any change to the form of the government into one acceptable to western politicians, as was made after 1945 in Germany and Japan, is unlikely to have any lasting results in an under-developed country.

The future of asymmetric warfare is extremely vague particularly as, in the age of air travel and the internet, countries can no longer be quarantined as Afghanistan was in the 19th century. However it certainly seems that such conflicts are best tackled by non-military means if at all possible, and any measures that reduce law and order will be self-defeating in the long run.

The Western Sahara War

Because of the vagueness of the definition of asymmetric warfare there have been many conflicts that could be described as such. However the war described here closely fits the 'ideal case' given earlier, and is all the more interesting for being between non-western powers, and cannot be regarded as some kind of adjunct of the Cold War.

The country currently known as 'Western Sahara' really came into existence as 'Spanish Sahara', a part of the Spanish Empire, at the start of the 20th Century. The Spanish also had small areas of protectorates in Morocco. Western Sahara is a territory running 660 miles along the Atlantic coast to the south of Morocco. It extends an approximate average of 200 miles inland and has land frontiers of 986 miles with Mauritania, 276 miles with Morocco and 19 with Algeria. It is largely infertile and the only good thing about it is some mineral wealth. This mostly takes the form of phosphate deposits at Bou Craa, or Bukra (the Arabic for 'tomorrow'). Bukra is 62 miles from the nearest port, which is really a two-mile pier, and the phosphates are carried there by conveyor belt. Work started in 1969 and had an initial annual production capacity of 3.7 million tons. This was a huge enterprise by any standards, one that some might think worth fighting a war over. The population are Sahrawis, to some extent distinct from Moroccans.

The Spanish were not very demanding masters and did not interfere with the Sahrawi nomadic and tribal way of life. Consequently the Sahrawis do not seem to have particularly objected to them until 1956 when, as a part of the struggles for independence that were sweeping North Africa, an 'Army of Liberation' was formed. This was quite easily destroyed in combined Spanish/French operations by 1958, and the peace of poverty returned to Spanish Sahara. It was not the colonial powers but Morocco that would bring war.

Soon after receiving independence from France, Morocco tried to embark on an expansionist policy but made little progress. A part of its motivation was simple nationalism, but a part was to destabilise the possibly revolutionary new government of Algeria. Morocco was a very conservative monarchy and its government dreaded new ideas. Its claim on the Algerian oasis of Tindouf was rebuffed in 1963 in a short war. Then its claim on Mauritania was halted by the Organisation of African Unity (OAU). Then Moroccan eyes fell on Spanish Sahara.

The extent to which the Moroccans had a legitimate claim over Spanish Sahara is a matter of opinion, but the claim was pressed deliberately as a unifying factor in Moroccan politics which had recently been disturbed by a number of coups. An external success was expected to enhance the standing of the government and bring stability. The International Court of Justice did not recognise the claim so the Moroccans organised a huge demonstration known as the 'Green March', and in October 1975 half a million people marched into Spanish Sahara. The Spanish troops did not resist, probably as General Franco was dying the senior officers were more interested in their political future than fighting a pointless colonial war. The marchers were withdrawn pending a political settlement. While the Moroccans were pressing their claim to Spanish Sahara the Mauritanians also decided they had a claim, partly based on suspicion of Moroccan aims. The upshot was that the Spanish agreed to leave in February 1976, leaving the territory to be administered jointly by Morocco and Mauritania, the Mauritanians taking roughly the southern third. No-one seems to have asked the Sahrawis what they wanted.

Unfortunately for the occupying powers because of the development of phosphate mining and the resultant small-scale urbanisation, changes had some across Sahrawi society and a definite national consciousness was stirring. So when the Moroccan and Mauritanian troops entered what was now called 'Western Sahara' the local independence movement was already partly formed. Polisario, an acronym of *Frente Popular para la Liberacion del Sahara y Rio de Oro* (The Popular Front for the Liberation of the Sahara and the Rio de Oro), was born in may 1973. It soon started attacking Spanish outposts, manned by local levies, the *Tropas Nomadas*, and in October 1974 it attacked and halted the phosphates conveyor belt as a kind of curtain raising spectacular.

When the Moroccan and Mauritanian forces occupied the country the Polisario forces, with 30,000 refugees, withdrew to Algeria. This was not easy, the Moroccans were alive to the threat posed by Polisario, and when it was withdrawing through the north of the country towards Algeria the Moroccan air force attacked it with napalm and phosphorous ordnance, causing heavy casualties. In one incident, among many, some Algerian troops, supplying aid to the refugees, had crossed the border into Western Sahara and were attacked by the Moroccans, taking heavy casualties. Less than three weeks later a Polisario unit attacked the 300 Moroccans posted there and massacred a large number of them.

Once the Sahrawis found a base in Algeria they prepared to fight back. In this they were helped by the Algerians who supplied them with Russian-made weapons and modern jeeps and other vehicles. Polisario could now mount hit-and-run raids, not only in Western Sahara but also in Morocco and Mauritania. Many Sahrawis flocked to join Polisario, particularly the now redundant *Tropas Nomadas*.

To gain recognition on the international stage Polisario proclaimed the 'Sahrawi Arab Democratic Republic', SADR, the new manifestation of Western Sahara, on 27th February 1976. This was really a declaration of war. The armed force was to be the Sahrawi People's Liberation Army, but it was usually referred to as 'Polisario'.

The accent of the first part of the war seems to have been against Mauritania. It was certainly a softer target than Morocco for a number of reasons. Politically it was suspicious of Moroccan aims and would have regarded the SADR as a useful buffer state. Economically it was weak and dependent on some iron ore mines which were at Zouerate, close to the border with Western Sahara. Militarily, the army was small, around 3,000 soldiers, and poorly equipped. Also it was badly motivated. A large percentage of the other ranks were negroes conscripted from the south of the country and resentful of being deployed in an inter-arab war in the north.

The Polisario troops, now highly mobile, raided into Mauritania, striking the Zouerate iron ore mines and the railway which carried the ore to a port. The railway was as vulnerable to the Sahrawi raiders as the Turkish Hejaz railway was to TE Lawrence's raiders six decades earlier. Zouerate itself had been fortified by a ditch, eleven feet deep and 35 miles long, which ran all round it. Its garrison was increased to 1,500 soldiers, but on 1st May 1977 the Mauritanian commander was away when the Polisario guerrillas raided the town. The troops would not fight. The attackers caused extensive damage before withdrawing, but also captured six French mining engineers. The disruption of production was a very significant blow for the government.

The raids became more numerous and ambitious, they even struck, probably pounding straight down the *Route du Mauritanie*, at Nouakchott, the Mauritanian capital, which was on the coast, 220 miles south of Western Sahara.

The war was going badly for Mauritania. Even though the army had been dramatically increased in size Polisario seemed to be able to raid at will. Consequently, although the Mauritanian government had shown a long-standing enmity to both Morocco and France, help was requested from both. Naturally Morocco wanted to keep Mauritania in the war, and France had her own reasons for wanting to support Morocco, and could use the capture of the engineers as an excuse, so thousands of Moroccan troops were flown into Zouerate and other posts close to the border, and the French mounted an aerial campaign against the raiders called Operation Lamantin.

Operation Lamantin certainly scored some early successes, and struck some Polisario mobile columns, but the guerrillas soon learned better camouflage, dispersion and night operations and, in the end, Operation Lamantin was a failure, as aerial operations in the context of sub-conventional warfare tend to be.

Despite all this assistance the Mauritanian army had had enough and some officers led a coup against the government. The new government withdrew its troops from Western Sahara and recognised the SADR. This was a tricky political process, there being so many Moroccan troops in Mauritania, and it took several months.

As the Mauritanian troops withdrew, Moroccans took their place. This expansion of the war placed a great strain on the Moroccan economy and was not popular, but internal dissent was ruthlessly suppressed. Also Morocco's international position became difficult. Many OAU countries recognised SADR so Morocco left the OAU. On the other hand many Gulf Arab states supported Morocco and supplied money to buy weapons which initial came from France, but later from the USA which was eager to place Morocco firmly in the western *bloc*.

The Polisario forces, having the run of the open desert could attack the Moroccans at will. Bukra was defended with an anti-AFV ditch, but that did not save it and phosphate production was halted for six years. The Moroccans garrisoned a large number of small posts in the eastern part of the country, but the troops were unenterprising and undertook little more than guard duties. They still, however, had to be supplied and Moroccan convoys became very vulnerable. Polisario units raided deep into Morocco, but only as far as they would receive support from a Sahrawi population, they did not raid unto Moorish or Berber territory.

As the war continued it became clear that the Moroccan army could not defeat Polisario who could attack from anywhere along the entire eastern side of the country. As a result of the damage and casualties suffered by the Moroccans they dramatically altered their tactics. In 1980 they decided to withdraw their garrisons facing the desert and to build a colossal field fortification running down the eastern side of the settled, fertile and productive part of Western Sahara to restrict Polisario to the desert areas. The parallel with Hadrian is obvious. This fortification was called the 'Berm'(see note), or sometimes the 'Moroccan Wall'. As has been seen, extensive field fortifications had been built at both Bukra and Zouerate. These fortifications do not seem to have been that effective, but lessons must have been learned from them.

By 1982 the Berm was over 250 miles (400 km) long and was effective in its aim. It was subject to modifications after this date and it was finally claimed to be 2,700 km long. The Berm runs along high ground, it consists of a wall, two metres high, built of sand and stone, backed by trenches and bunkers. At five kilometre intervals there are platoon bases and section posts scattered between them. Around four kilometres behind the wall are the larger bases of mobile units with tanks and other AFVs, and artillery positions. In front of the wall is a minefield that runs along the wall's entire length. Close behind the wall is a series of radar posts which gives a contiguous picture of and movement on Polisario's side of the Berm to a range of up to 80 km, information being passed to the artillery. Construction only ended in 1987.

The Berm achieved its aim of keeping Polisario out but the expense was colossal. To a large extent the cost of the Berm and the war in general was met by Saudi Arabia, but there can be little doubt that the economy of Morocco suffered badly. It has been estimated that the number of troops required to man it was equal to the entire Sahrawi population. The situation became unsupportable for both parties. Polisario was restricted to the infertile east of the country, and Morocco could not afford the war. Consequently a cease-fire was signed in September 1991. However to date a complete political settlement has not been reached, the SADR is still on the UN list of 'non-self-governing territories', and the whole sorry episode is taking the form of a running sore that can still claim many more victims.

Note

This is a modern use of the term. A berm was originally the space left between a castle's wall and the moat. It provided a walk for sentries but its greatest purpose was to prevent rubble from the wall falling into the moat. Keeping the rubble on the berm would preserve the moat as an obstacle and provide a little protection for the wall from the attacker's artillery. Over the years the term has evolved into an imprecise one indicating any kind of embanked field fortification.

9

Nuclear Warfare

Nuclear weapons derive their destructive power from nuclear reactions. The first such weapons, Atomic Bombs, used the fission of, usually, plutonium. Later bombs, Hydrogen Bombs, used the fusion of derivatives of hydrogen, a process which is started, in effect, by an atom bomb.

The first, and only, uses of nuclear bombs in war was in 1945 when one each was dropped by conventional bombers on the Japanese cities of Hiroshima and Nagasaki. The result was the destruction of these cities and the immediate deaths of around 120,000 people. Many more were to die later either of wounds or radiation. The Atomic bombs used were rated as 20 Kilotons, that is as effective as 20,000 tons of TNT.

As horrifying as this was similar casualties had been caused by the carpet bombing of Japanese cities, which were built largely of wood and other easily combustible materials, so the Atomic Bombs were regarded as just super-conventional weapons. Consequently the revolution nuclear weapons were to cause in international affairs was not immediately obvious. However when, in 1949, the USSR tested its first nuclear bomb, it could be seen that previous assumptions had become obsolete.

Since 1945 there has been no actual use of nuclear weapons, therefore nuclear strategy has depended on the development of new weapons, and their means of delivery to their targets, and the evolution of the best methods of using them. The overwhelming bulk of nuclear weapons deployment has occurred in the context of the Cold War, the history of which will be considered in the next section. Here basic principles only will be considered.

Nuclear weapons are of two different kinds, Battlefield and

Strategic. Battlefield nuclear weapons are comparatively small and are delivered by missiles or artillery pieces. In general the use of these weapons should favour the defending side, and they are most likely to be used at the start of a retreat. They can have various effects. 'Neutron Bombs' produce radiation which will penetrate armour and kill troops in AFVs, but be relatively ineffective against buildings. 'Salted Bombs' will produce high levels of radiation which will contaminate large areas and make them uncrossable, and ordinary airburst hydrogen bombs will be devastating against troops in the open.

The use of battlefield nuclear weapons is more problematic than might seem at first sight. During the later, static, part of the Korean War the US Army set up an 'Atomic Committee' to consider the use of these weapons. The committee reported back that they were of little tactical value, even though the Chinese could not reply in kind.

This last consideration points to the great disadvantage attached to battlefield nuclear weapons in that that using one will cross a threshold and, it can be confidently predicted, will result in a larger one being sent back, and very fast escalation until large strategic weapons are launched.

The use of strategic nuclear weapons depends on two basic concepts, first and second strike. A first strike capacity is the ability to destroy the opponent's nuclear weapons before they can be used. A second strike capacity is the ability to hit the enemy's population centres. The essence of deterrence is to convince the enemy that the defenders will always be able to retain a second strike capacity. This was difficult to do when the method of delivery was manned bombers which could be hit on the ground or intercepted in flight by missiles or fighters, but once long range missiles had been developed, it became feasible. Missiles can be stored in, and launched from, hardened sites, or fired from mobile platforms, such as railway wagons, which can be difficult to locate. Once a missile has been launched there is no practical defence against it, particularly as the more sophisticated missiles can carry ten independently-targeted warheads.

Of course if the defenders, having weathered the first strike, then deploy their second strike and destroy the enemy's cities, they can expect the same back. This is referred to as Mutual Assured Destruction, MAD, and the peace resulting from the fear of it was known as the 'balance of terror'.

The Soviet government adopted a number of measures designed to reduce the effects of a strike against its cities, such as public shelters and stores of food. How effective such measures would have been is open to discussion. The US government has not followed suit.

In general it could be held that the existence of nuclear weapons has resulted in the obsolescence of major conventional warfare among the major powers. But the world cannot be blasé about this threat, and as progressively more nations are acquiring these weapons, predictions would be rash. In the Kargil War the Indians and the Pakistanis are believed to have ensured that the conflict did not spread because both sides had nuclear weapons, and by forcing moderation this might be regarded as encouraging. This is because of what the Israelis call the 'Sampson Option'. Probably the most convincing current scenario for the use of nuclear weapons is by a secondary power as an act of desperation when losing a conventional war. In such a case its possession of nuclear weapons may well be its insurance that the super-powers must come to its aid if it were suffering a great defeat.

Also the existence of a weapons program, involving ballistic missiles and rumours of nuclear research, will deter outside interference in a country's affairs. It is noticeable that it was because of Colonel Gadaffi's surrender of his weapons program that NATO and the United States were at liberty to take action against Libya. Possibly more importantly all the highly publicised inspections of Iraq, looking for nuclear weapons, can be seen as a means of ensuring that it would be safe for the US-UK coalition to invade. The fact is that no country armed with nuclear weapons has ever been invaded, a point that will not have been lost on several countries that find themselves at odds with the USA.

So far nuclear weapons have been considered in terms of conventional war, but the march of science has produced a potentially terrifying scenario in that nuclear weapons can now be made small enough to be deployed by terrorist organisations. How this will work out in practice only the future will tell.

The Cold War

The Cold War can be regarded as the inevitable result of the USSR pursuing the centuries-old Russian expansionist foreign policy, and coming up against European countries backed by the economic might of the USA. Alternatively it can be regarded as the inevitable result of the Second World War. The end of which saw the destruction of the Euro-centric system of diplomacy which had been built up over the centuries, and world power largely divided between two super-powers, the USA and the USSR. Either way the two super-powers dominated the post-war world.

Despite their wartime alliance these super-powers naturally tended to be suspicious of each other, a suspicion based on their own view of the world and plans for the future.

The USA, still smarting from Pearl Harbour, was determined never again to be the victim of a surprise attack, consequently wanted some military bases around the world, and would never again allow her armed forces to atrophy as was the case pre-war. She would be suspicious of any state becoming too powerful; too powerful, that is, by American standards. She would encourage world prosperity via free trade.

The USSR, having endured staggering casualties in the war, was even more worried about the possibility of a surprise attack than was the USA, so insisted on covering her western flank with buffer states over which she exerted rigid political control. However the most important factor of Soviet politics was the very nature of the political system. One of the basic tenets of socialism is the coming clash with capitalism. Add to that the paranoia of Stalinism and the result is a philosophy of government looking for enemies.

Also, because of the spirit of the time, and wartime propaganda, the populations of the super-powers believed wholeheartedly in the values and visions of their governments.

With these differences between the super-powers it is not surprising that they found many things to disagree about. To an extent the Russian bitterness started in 1943 with Stalin demanding a second front (invasion of Europe). He could point out that the eastern front was tying down 80% of the Axis forces at colossal cost, and had little sympathy with British and US difficulties. Even the dispatch of billions of dollars worth of military aid did not mollify him.

At the Yalta conference, in February 1945, basic disputes were not resolved. Britain and the US surrendered Poland to the Soviets because they had no realistic alternative. The Soviets pledged to encourage democracy and liberalism, but they had no intention of doing either.

The major disagreement was over the future of Germany. The Soviets wanted a very repressive policy designed to screw out of Germany the last pfennig of reparations. The US seems to have been a little vague, starting with something like the Lindemann Plan, but coming round to the view that a German economic recovery would be good for the world in general.

Soon after the destruction of Hiroshima and Nagasaki,

following a short period of friendly relations, Soviet governmental paranoia reasserted itself and, as Winston Churchill put it, an 'Iron Curtain' descended around the USSR and its client states.

It is true that the Soviets were behaving in a repressive way in Eastern Europe. This was not surprising considering the brutal nature of the fighting on the eastern front. When Soviet troops reached the first German towns, like Nemmersdorf and Striegau, they massacred everyone, and looted everything, they could. With precedents like these, countries occupied by the Red Army could expect the worst.

Despite this, the real worry for the western allies was the sharp rise in popularity of far left politics in both Western Europe and the colonies. The USA answered all this with the Truman Doctrine and the Marshal Plan.

The Truman Doctrine was the pledge of the USA to support any nation fighting against a communist takeover. It soon had its successes in Greece and Turkey. The Marshal Plan was the offer of US financial aid to European countries, providing that they would run their economies in an approved manner. Western European countries were enthusiastic, but the USSR felt that it was a plan to weaken its grip on its satellites and would have nothing to do with it.

The reception of the Marshal Plan really showed how Europe was now divided into two camps, or rival spheres of influence. It was followed, in February 1948, by a communist coup in Czechoslovakia which was henceforward in the communist camp. Then came the blockade of Berlin, which seems in retrospect to have been pointless provocation. It evoked the Berlin Airlift and turned out to be a propaganda disaster for Stalin who soon called it off.

The tense situation in Europe resulted in NATO, the North Atlantic Treaty Organisation, being set up. This was a mutual security pact including not only most of the western

European countries but also the USA and Canada. Locking the USA into European defence turned out to be one of the greatest triumphs of 20th century statesmanship.

Scarcely had NATO sprung into existence when the Korean War broke out and sparked a hysterical fear of a vast communist plot. Many troops in Europe were sent to the far east, then it was noticed that the USSR and satellites had over 170 divisions that could be deployed against NATO. This dwarfed the NATO figure which, despite best efforts, only reached 25 by 1960. The vast bulk of the communist units were divisions in name only, actually being only small cadres and maintenance crews. It is difficult to know how much this was appreciated at the time.

The Korean War evoked an illustration of the limits of the use of the threat of the 'Bomb' as a means of diplomatic pressure. When General MacArthur wanted pressure brought to bear on China, Mao Tse-Tung famously dismissed the bomb as "*a paper tiger....China has millions of people. The deaths of 10m to 20m people is nothing to be afraid of.*" Perhaps it is just as well that the US had no interest in widening the war. General MacArthur was recalled soon after.

If the Bomb had little strategic use it did seem that it might have a tactical application. But, as already mentioned, the committee set up by the US army to consider this reported that atomic weapons were of little tactical value in Korea, and by implication, anywhere else.

The perceived difficulties in the use of atomic, and nuclear, weapons natural resulted in the strengthening of NATO forces. The USSR responded, in 1955, by setting up the Warsaw Pact, which formalised its control over its European satellites.

By this time the USSR had caught up with the USA in that it had tested some Hydrogen bombs. This started the nuclear arms race which is usually regarded as the salient feature of the Cold War.

Initially the USSR was not capable of delivering its nuclear weapons to the USA, but the US, with a series of long range bombers could strike the USSR, so the Americans were content with a policy of 'Massive Retaliation' against Soviet cities. There was also, despite known difficulties, a plan to use small nuclear weapons in a tactical context to try to even up the massive disparity in numbers of NATO and Warsaw Pact troops.

By the end of the 1950s the USA was winning the nuclear arms race, and could hit nearly all Soviet territory with massive bombs carried by intercontinental ballistic missiles against which there was no realistic defence. The Soviets could not match this and their answer was to move their missiles closer to the USA. This evoked the Cuban Missile Crisis of 1962, during which international tension reached a peak, when the Soviets placed some medium range missiles within 90 miles of the USA. Fortunately following a few threats they withdrew them, and the US withdrew some missiles they had placed in Turkey.

There is no doubt that the Cuban crisis caused a pause for thought. In the next year the 'hot line' between the White House and the Kremlin was installed, and a partial test ban treaty signed. These were, it is true, small steps, but although the world was still living under the threat of Mutual Assured Destruction, some of the venom seems to have gone out of the confrontation.

One reason for this was that neither side managed to create a reliable first strike capacity. Without such a capacity nuclear warfare was pointless. Nuclear weapons were deployed in large numbers to achieve 'strategic superiority', which has been described as more overkill than the enemy. As Henry Kissinger remarked, "*one of the questions we have to ask ourselves as a country is what in the name of God is strategic superiority? What do you do with it?"* These were questions not that easy to answer.

There was, of course, a second way of triggering Massive Retaliation and that was via battlefield nuclear weapons. Both NATO and the Warsaw Pact constantly developed and practised tactics to make the best use of these, or, in NATO's case, to make their use unnecessary. However there can be little doubt that, whatever the effect of these was on the tactical situation, their use would cause a very fast escalation to MAD.

There have been three occasions when requests for the use of small nuclear weapons have reached the President of the USA. In the first General MacArthur wanted them in Korea. In 1954 the French asked for them at Dien-Bien-Phu, and thirdly, General Westmoreland, in superficially similar circumstances, asked for them at Khe Sanh. It is impossible to believe that any of these requests was taken seriously in Washington.

Another reason for the reduced tension was that China was taking over from the USSR as the USA's most feared enemy. In fact even during the Vietnam war, with China aiding and abetting North Vietnam, and the USSR publicly sympathising, the US and the USSR were inching towards nuclear detente.

Detente, which flowered during the late 1960s and the early 1970s was certainly not the end of the nuclear arms race but it was an organised and managed confrontation. Remarkably each side had military missions roving around in the other's territory observing manoeuvres and the like. Also President Johnson was planning to visit Moscow, but the trip was called off after the invasion of Czechoslovakia.

Detente and a general reduction of tension suited both sides. The USSR was also having trouble with China, and the US was in financial trouble brought on by the Vietnam war.

When Nixon took over the presidency he made a point of making friendly contact with China, hoping to play China and the USSR off against each other. To some extent this worked, showing how ideology always takes second place behind *realpolitik*.

There were, naturally, ups and downs, but a Strategic Arms Limitation Treaty, SALT I, was signed on 26th May 1972 and this was followed by a big increase in US/USSR trade. The next step, SALT II, was being pursued, but 'Watergate' and the following election slowed things down.

In Europe a significant thaw occurred following the decision of the West German Chancellor, Willy Brandt, to recognise East Germany and the *de facto* borders. Even so the nuclear confrontation did not slow down, and the Soviets deployed their latest missile, the SS20, in Europe. Worse, a series of events round the world occurred, each of which looked like a US defeat. These can be briefly listed as: the fall of South Vietnam, the early stages of the Angolan war, the Sandinistas' victory in Nicaragua, the Iran hostage crisis, and the Soviet invasion of Afghanistan. Perhaps it is no wonder that a pessimistic Henry Kissinger looking at future prospects commented *"first we lose the conventional war, then we lose the tactical nuclear exchange. Then we blow up the world"*.

However it must be noted that during this list of disasters SALT II was signed.

The invasion of Afghanistan was really the end of detente, though to some extent the American reaction was based on a misapprehension. The Soviets regarded their actions as purely defensive. The situation in Afghanistan throughout 1979 was becoming chaotic. This was bad enough but it was judged that the end result might be an anti-Soviet regime, and the USSR, having invested heavily in Afghanistan, moved to prevent that. The US regarded the invasion as the first move in a campaign to dominate the Persian Gulf. They answered it by an increase in military spending, an embargo on grain exports to the USSR, expanded trade with China, and the deployment of Pershing II and Cruise missiles in Europe.

Next year, 1980, Ronald Reagan was elected president and the Cold War became even more intense. Military spending went up again, planning started on the Strategic Defence Initiative anti-missile defence system, Grenada was invaded and aid was sent to the Afghan guerrillas fighting the Soviet occupying forces. Fighting back against Soviet influence at the very limits of its reach was to become the essential aspect of what was to be called the 'Reagan Doctrine'.

The Strategic Defence Initiative (Star Wars) was particularly worrying to the Soviets. It was actually only at the planning stage in 1983, but the US government was 'talking it up' and the Soviets chose to believe them. If it had been fully functional it would have robbed the USSR of any second strike capability and given the USA what could have been the decisive edge in a nuclear exchange. Consequently it is not surprising that the Soviets broke off the on-going arms limitation talks.

After 1980 the structure of the super-power confrontation started to weaken. In that year the non-communist Polish trade union 'Solidarity' challenged the political establishment, and when the USSR tried to mobilise reservists to invade Poland the system broke down in chaos. The Afghan war was unpopular and this was having a bad effect on the attitude of Soviet citizens to their government.

However even if it might seem that the super-powers were on the verge of war, in Europe east-west relations were still cordial, and when the USA demanded sanctions against the USSR, the western European countries would not join in. While western governments were behaving like this their people held a series of huge anti-nuclear rallies that no elected politician could ignore. Putting all this together it is not surprising that arms limitation talks started again in 1985, at first with Chernenko then, after his death, with Mikhail Gorbachev.

The accession to power of Mikhail Gorbachev was really the beginning of the end of the Cold War. Maintaining the horizontal confrontation with the USA was no longer sustaining the cohesion of the USSR, and the danger of vertical warfare within the union was becoming real. He realised that the USSR had more urgent things to do, and better things to spend its money on, than a nuclear arms race. He also knew that no-one was going to invade Russia. Unfortunately there was one potential danger in his liberalising regime. The USSR, as a super-national government, would be weakened and this could result in several former Soviet Socialist Republics declaring their independence which the USSR could not allow. The example of Chechnya has been given in Chapter 3. It could be that many of the citizens of such republics sigh for the days of Cold War and stability.

The nuclear confrontation of the super-powers in Europe was the most well known aspect of the Cold War, but outside Europe the Cold War can be reckoned to have claimed many millions of lives. It is impossible to give a reliable figure as most of the conflicts involved would have occurred regardless of the Cold War, but the Cold War resulted in vast supplies of arms and sometimes changed the nature and scale of these conflicts.

The standard scenario was that a conflict would start up, then one of the super-powers would, hoping to gain some advantage, start supplying one side, then the other super-power, usually not being interested in the original conflict but just wanting to prevent the other gaining that advantage, would come to the rescue of the other side.

In 1947 the USA adopted the Truman Doctrine, and the Soviet response was formalised by Nikita Khrushchev in

1961 when he pledged support for peoples fighting wars of 'National Liberation'.

One of the USA's priorities was to see the European empires closed down and the colonial governments replaced, ideally, by pro-western democratic governments. Great Britain, accepting the inevitable, supported this aim, France and the Netherlands for a while did not. Consequently when, after the communists had gained control of China and there was a danger of a large communist bloc forming, the USA, not wanting to alienate France and the Netherlands who were vital in Europe, did not always follow its preferred policy. This ultimately led to their sending troops to South Vietnam.

Several cases have been mentioned in previous chapters of the super-powers taking sides in a conflict, the most important being the Arab-Israeli wars, but the nature of such cases changed in the 1980s when the USSR started sending troops into third world countries, Angola, Ethiopia and Afghanistan. This stood Khrushchev's pledge on its head, and the latter case did its bit to end the Cold War.

In general the way in which the European confrontation was extended into other, usually third world, countries was non-productive, murderous, and a shameful chapter in world history.

The Cold War necessitated the growth of a huge arms industry and bureaucracy to support it. In the USA they were characterised as the 'military-industrial complex' by President Eisenhower and they became a political force demanding ever higher defence expenditure. It must be noted that even though the Cold War is over, the military-industrial complex in the USA has not been significantly reduced in size or cost.

10

How Wars End

Wars don't last forever and, ultimately, each must end. There are four ways this can happen:

Unconditional Surrender,
Negotiation,
Fading Away,
Foreign Intervention.

As with other lists of categories involved in the study of war these categories are not mutually exclusive, and the end of a particular war may be described in terms of two or three of them. This list is valid for both vertical and horizontal warfare, though the form is different for each.

Vertical wars will be considered first.

Usually a war ending with an unconditional surrender will see the incumbent government being replaced by the insurgents'. However it is possible that the government could win and this could involve the destruction of the insurgent movement by wholesale massacre, as seems to have been the case in some Central American countries.

A negotiated settlement will see the insurgents entering legitimate politics and giving up violence. At the time of writing this seems to be the route being followed by the Provisional IRA and the Basque Separatist Organisation ETA.

An insurgency can be said to be fading away when its level of violence can be contained by the civilian police. This stage is reached when the rank-and-file members accept defeat, or at least the failure of the armed struggle. This feeling of defeat is increased if the leaders enter politics and hence grow rich. This is usually seen as an act of betrayal by the rest and may decisively hurt their morale. However the government will be aware that the insurgency could well break out again and will make a series of concessions to the defeated party to prevent this.

Except in the case of a classic *coup d'état* both the government and the insurgents will be, to one degree or another, dependent upon foreign assistance. The providers of this assistance, paying the piper can call the tune, and often do. When Cuba stopped supplying aid to the San Salvadoran insurgency that insurgency was finished, but just as significantly the USA which had been supporting the government could use its position to insist on it improving its appalling 'human rights' behaviour.

All these cases will see the withdrawal of foreign troops fighting for the government, and a Vietnamisation-type program carried out. Whether this is a symptom of success or failure will depend on the individual case.

In the case of horizontal warfare there is greater emphasis on the peace treaty. The terms of which must be seen as reasonable by the population of the defeated side or the situation will remain unstable, possibly for generations.

There is not so much difference between unconditional surrender and a negotiated settlement as might at first seem the case. Unconditional surrender would seem to be as conclusive as possible, but the case not being one of primary warfare, and the losers not being massacred, they will remain and expect reasonable treatment. After 1945 once the initial horrors of shortages and population relocation had passed West Germany was well treated by any standards and became stable and prosperous. Conversely East Germany was not well treated and became the opposite. Even the Russian occupation of the Baltic States, which at the time must have seemed as crushing as unconditional surrender could be, was a failure in the long term. Long term occupations will only succeed if the occupiers and the occupied become allies against an external threat. This was the post-war situation in West Germany. Otherwise occupation will inhibit industrial development and foster nationalist resentment.

The occupation of a defeated country and its government by the victors, sometimes for many years, is a necessity if the requirement is to effect a total change in its polity and behaviour. This was achieved after the Second World War in West Germany and Japan, however, at the time of writing, there is some question as to the degree of success in the cases of Iraq and Afghanistan. Soldiers, it seems, prefer kinetic solutions to nation building!

Wars can end in a negotiated settlement. The negotiations are usually set up by a third party, and can, if not rigorously chaired, become exercises in propaganda and political posturing. Nations will only enter negotiations when it is obvious that there is little to gain by further fighting. This might come about because one side has achieved its limited war aim, or because the fighting has reached a stalemate, as in Korea. At the end of that war it took two years of intense negotiations just to get the armistice signed.

Negotiations can take a long time to get started. The step down from war to peace is just too large for politicians, or people, to lightly countenance as it would involve an element of admitting defeat, and no-one wants to be the first to do that. The great danger in this is that, as defeat looms, there might be an urge to escalate the conflict by launching nuclear weapons, the 'Sampson Option'.

Naturally the worse the military situation, the harsher will be the terms accepted by the losing side. If the terms were seen to be too mild then there might be a rumble of discontent from the victor's population, and the loser's may be happy to go a second round, as was the case over Schleswig-Holstein in the 19th century. It is all a matter of public perception.

A settlement will be agreed on when one of the belligerents is prepared to make such concessions as would make the war no longer worthwhile for the other. Concessions are more difficult to make the more involved with the war effort the population is, and the military situation must be that much more desperate before they are offered. This was why the two World Wars ground on so remorselessly. A government might be driven to making concessions purely by the military situation, by economic difficulties, by diplomatic pressure or world opinion, or as a result of its own population withdrawing its support for the war. This latter case is most worrying for the government as it makes its own position less secure, and can even lead to a revolution, as in Russia in 1917. Naturally the government which has the tightest control of its people will have a great advantage in negotiations.

The case of the German wars is the obvious illustration of how poor peace treaties can have disastrous results.

The German victory in the Franco-Prussian War of 1870-71 resulted in the creation of the German Empire. This evoked a wave of '*Hurrah Patriotisimus*', and to propitiate this, despite his own lack of enthusiasm, Bismarck annexed Alsace and Lorraine.

The French resented this loss and this resentment was a significant factor in sustaining the national animosity that brought about the Great War.

The treaty ending the Great War brought humiliation, depression and great hardship on the Germans and ultimately made the NSDAP look like Germany's great hope.

All this shows that, although everyone would agree that the only legitimate war aim is a better state of peace, the question is always, for whom? It would take a great statesman to see beyond the narrow aspirations of his own country to the greater benefits of the whole interlinked world. Unfortunately such statesmen were missing in 1871 and 1919.

Ideally each nation should have a place in the world order commensurate with its population, natural resources and industrial capacity, and its armed forces may be used to guarantee this. But if a nation has a greater place in the world that its population, natural resources and industrial capacity are worth, but retains that place solely by the actual or potential use of armed force, the result will be an unstable, and usually short, peace.

Peace treaties are usually imposed on the weaker side and few governments have achieved a sensible negotiated end to the fighting. One of these was the Chinese in its 1962 clash with the Indians. They got their logistics right, beat the Indian troops, showed that they could invade India if they wanted, then withdrew and normalized relations. The world should learn from this.

The defeat of one side is sometimes accompanied by a regime change. This can work out quite well as the victor will not want to say that his quarrel was with the defeated population, but only with the government, so negotiations should proceed fairly amicably. However that should not be relied on. In 1918 the Kaiser abdicated and left Germany, but this did not save Germany from a crushing peace settlement. Seeing this it was not surprising that there was no particular movement to get rid of Hitler's government in the last months of the Second World War, it would have made no difference.

If the war had been undertaken by the aggressors to either alter the victim nation's government or at least the policy of the government, it will withdraw its troops once it has achieved that end. However it is possible that the defeated country's population will not be happy with the new situation which, after a few years, could revert to that obtaining before the war. This may result in another invasion being felt necessary, and the whole process repeating.

In this context it is apposite to quote Maximilien Robespierre:

> *"The most extraordinary idea ever to take origin in the head of a politician is the notion that it is enough for the armed people to invade another people in order to move the invaded population to adopt the laws and constitution of the invading people. No-one loves armed missionaries, and the first piece of advice offered by nature and caution is that invaders should be repelled as enemies."*

Some small scale wars do not have neat endings but just fade away. This usually happens when one side has achieved at least one of its tactical objectives and continuation of the war would involve substantial escalation. Alternatively circumstances for a country might change and other courses of action become more important than continuing the war. This is one way of looking at the Soviet defeat in the Cold War. Handling financial problems, Militant Islam, and the demands for independence of many of the Soviet Republics became more important than maintaining the confrontation with NATO.

Two examples follow of short conventional wars that did not end with a negotiated peace: the Falklands War and the Gulf campaign of 1991.

In 1982 the Argentinians invaded the Falklands and established themselves there. The British sent two brigades that forced them back to the Argentine. The Argentinian people then staged an uprising and deposed General Galtieri and established a more liberal regime. There has been a little bit of political noise since, but in general that was that.

In 1990 the Iraqis invaded Kuwait and established themselves there. A coalition of interested nations sent a large army, built around a US contingent, to Saudi-Arabia, and in February the next year drove the Iraqis out. However

197

after the campaign, because of the unstable situation, it was necessary to keep large forces in the area, to enforce the sanctions policy and to maintain 'No Fly' zones over large parts of Iraq. This was a result of the Saddam Hussein regime emerging from the war actually stronger and more stable that it was at the start. The main prop of the regime, the Republican Guard, had not been touched by the war, but the army, a potential rival for power, had been largely destroyed.

The upshot of this was that in 2003 the US, with the support of the UK, invaded Iraq. This invasion was, at the time, justified on amazingly specious grounds. Occupying Iraq turned out to be very easy, but it did not take too long before the Iraqis started to resent the presence of foreign, non-Muslim, troops in their country and started attacking them. The troops spent years carrying out internal security operations, while, under this impetus, the threat of terrorism throughout the rest of the world drastically increased.

The interlinked nature of the world-wide system of states and their general requirement for peace and stability mean that they usually bring pressure to bear on belligerent states to stop fighting. On occasion, it may be suspected, this pressure is not unwelcome. For example in the closing phase of the *Yom Kippur* Arab-Israeli war of 1973 the Israelis had crossed the Suez canal and seemed to be making triumphal progress towards Cairo. Actually their logistic situation was potentially disastrous, relying on a small number of highly vulnerable pontoon bridges across the canal. So, when they were asked, they were glad to stop.

There is a further category of peace settlement, not listed above, that is hardly relevant in the modern world but was essential during the empire building period of history. This involved the annexation of the defeated country into the empire. The war might then change from being a horizontal one to a vertical one as the native population fought against the new civilian administration.

If the war has been in any way protracted then munitions production will have been a concern to the government, and this will have resulted in many concessions and promises being made to organised labour. Unfortunately the end of a war must be accompanied by a reduction in public spending. This is apt to bring on a trade depression and a feeling of disillusion as the government is seen to renege on many of its promises. The economic run-down following a war is an inevitable part of that war and must be carefully controlled. This is particularly true if the war has taken the form of a revolution.

Similarly if the war approached totality then it is almost inevitable that the government will observe the superb production achieved by the mobilisation of labour, command economy and wartime spirit, and try to retain these in peacetime. This may be tried through the worthy motivation of building a country fit for heroes, or just being reluctant to relinquish power. Either way, wartime command economies do not work in peace time and sooner or later this will become apparent to the detriment of government-people relations.

11

The Morality of War

War is a very human activity often evoking intense passion and arguments about its morality. Unfortunately these arguments usually become inconclusive, arcane and irrelevant to realities. This chapter will consider morality as it affects the conduct of war.

People either individually or as part of a group, like to feel that they are acting morally, or at least not immorally. This feeling might be purely instinctive and subconscious, or it might be carefully thought out, but it certainly exists.

War is a system for killing people. Therefore, providing the sanctity of human life is accepted, war must always be morally wrong except in two rare instances of the 'Volume of Harm' concept, one being a successful war preventing wholesale massacre, for example if a war had been launched to prevent Pol Pot killing a large percentage of the population of Cambodia. The second case being a war declared to prevent a sequence of events that would cause more casualties than the preventive war being declared. These cases are very similar and the justification in both cases is the same, that the war ultimately saves lives.

They will also be very rare, consequently most wars are immoral and that obtains for both sides. It is possible that since the Thirty Years War the vast majority of educated people has recognised this. However experience has shown that wars will happen and, to an extent this might not be a bad thing as a large number of secondary wars might provide a safety valve preventing pressure building up for a primary war. Consequently, in the years following the near-primary devastation of the Thirty Years War a set of customs was established designed to make warfare as limited and as humane as possible.

The essence of these customs was that civilians took no part in war, but were liable to be taxed by the victors, and soldiers did not pillage civilians. Nothing is perfect, and on many occasions soldiers had to forage to live, and sometimes wholesale pillage and destruction was a method of bringing pressure to bear on a government, as shown when Marlborough's soldiers destroyed parts of Bavaria before the Battle of Blenheim. Despite this the system worked well.

The real problem appeared half-way through the nineteenth century when peacetime conscription became standard, first in Prussia, then in the rest of Germany, then in most of Europe. Conscription resulted in armies becoming 'Nations in Arms', yet governments dreaded the primary warfare that this implied and the subsequent loss of control. Consequently a series of international conventions agreed on an elaborate set of rules regulating the conduct of war. As the early days of the Great War showed this system worked, providing civilians could be kept out of the fighting.

This was well appreciated by the Germans who undertook a policy of reprisals in the event of attack on their troops by Belgian and French civilians. This policy was termed *Schrecklichkeit,* frightfulness, and in the short term it worked though it is doubtful how much damage a few militia men and *francs-tireurs* could have done to the large German army. In the long term it gave a vast propaganda boost to the Allies. The Germans, of course, like everyone else, had expected a short war.

The same thinking influenced German policy when they invaded the USSR in 1941. They knew that the distances to be covered would be huge and they would not have the troops to guard their communications, consequently they decided that any guerrilla actions would be met by horrifying reprisals. The Germans knew the limitations of this kind of policy but, once again, they expected the Russian campaign to be over in three months, and planned for their reprisals policy to keep the occupied areas quiet just that long.

Both cases of frightfulness were ultimately self-defeating, and judged to be highly immoral by their opponents. They cleared the way for an escalation of immoral behaviour, a concept which is particularly applicable in vertical wars.

It is interesting to note that the wars that have been most generally approved of since 1945 were the Falklands campaign and the Six Day war of 1967. In both cases the fighting took place, in moorland and desert, where there were no civilians.

As a war proceeds the soldiers tend to settle down with a reasonable code of battlefield conduct, they have everything to gain by fostering a spirit of reciprocity, but the war in general will have a degrading effect on the societies fighting it.

Naturally, belligerent governments deny this, usually quoting the immorality of the other side, and the long-term good to follow from their own actions. They will find the people easier to convince if they feel insulted in any way, or that National Honour has been insulted. A consideration of how many lives and how much suffering and sorrow such insults are worth will not be raised.

Morality is comparative. An essential aspect of the Western Allies' strategy in the Second World War was the bombing of Axis cities. After the war this would have been regarded as a terrible war crime except that in the last few weeks of the war the troops had come across places like Belsen. The one horror more than cancelled out the other.

A defensive war, when the enemy is actually within the defender's country, will usually be regarded as highly moral, even if the government is unpopular with the people. This was the case with the USSR when the Germans invaded in 1941, and yet it still became the 'Great Patriotic War'.

Similarly when US and UK forces invaded Iraq in 2003 the

Iraqi army, disillusioned with their government, did not fight but just faded away. Quite soon a lot of other Iraqis did fight.

Moral considerations revolve around the war aims and the conduct of the fighting.

The morality of a war is almost never considered by a government launching it. There is often plenty of talk about an Ethical Foreign Policy, but actual warfare comes down to *Realpolitik*. Morality is invoked later as an excuse. A good war is a huge boost to a politician's ego and popularity. This will be more important to him than any worries about morality.

The armed forces concern themselves to only a small extent with the morality of the aim of the war that they are called on to fight. This is quite reasonable, the forces should obey the government's orders and stay out of political discussions. However the forces must conduct the actual fighting in as ethical a way as possible, which they will want to do to encourage a spirit of reciprocity with the enemy.

Finally the people, and the unfortunate and indisputable truth is that people in general like to be at war. Being at war poses no real threat to the overwhelming majority of the population and it adds a *frisson* of enjoyable excitement and meaning to the boring lives of working people. This was reflected by the results of a study carried out in the USA which showed that the number of civilian suicides declined during the Second World War. A large number of people actually benefit from a war. These will include industrialists who manufacture munitions, their employees who go on overtime and career servicemen who will be promoted up the ranks of expanding military organisations. In all these cases and many more, those involved will justify their acceptance of the war through its supposed morality.

The reaction of the public was strikingly demonstrated during the Great War. Initially public enthusiasm was driven by unthinking patriotism. Soon atrocity propaganda resulted in the war being a fight for civilisation which had to be supported. Then, as the war became total and almost everyone was involved in it at one level or another, the previously divided and class-ridden societies found a great enthusiasm for common endeavour. It might be supposed that this enthusiasm came from above via government propaganda, but simple observation shows that this was not so. Even now antique and curio shops sell large numbers of wartime postcards and ornaments. These were produced in such huge numbers because manufacturers knew that there was a market for them, and this was independent of the government.

This last point shows an unfortunate effect of public enthusiasm. In the first two stages mentioned above it could be controlled by the government; in the last, much less so. This was a contributory factor in the rejection of calls for a negotiated peace.

Criticism of a war's morality may start for a small number of people with a consideration of the war aims, but for the mass of the population it will start with their not agreeing with the actions of the troops. The perception of immorality can have a corrosive effect on public support for a long drawn-out war, as was demonstrated by the reaction of the US population to the war in Vietnam. This type of reaction seems strongest among western nations. In the Vietnam war the actions of US troops were closely scrutinised and criticised whereas atrocities carried out by communist forces, for example the massacre of approximately 5,000 civilians at Hue during the Tet offensive, were largely ignored. There is no doubt that the actions of the Vietnamese meant little to the American people, whereas they could identify with the US troops, and as they disapproved of their actions they withdrew their support for the war.

A very important aspect of the American people's reaction to the Vietnam war was that it was televised. Images of warfare and its horrors were there for all to see. Such considerations as this will increase rapidly as the information revolution proceeds apace.

The Vietnam experience shows how the perception of the morality of a war can change. This will occur firstly with a feeling of unease over the methods being used, then to questioning the basic war aims. This process can be followed in the Anglo-Irish war. Few people in Britain would have been interested had the war gone smoothly, but the activities of the Blacks and Tans, and other security forces, forced people to take notice, then they began questioning the morality of British policy. This was one of the factors resulting in the British government admitting defeat. The IRA did not beat the security forces; as a senior IRA man said, it was the British people who did it for them.

It follows then that the morality of a war is less likely to be questioned if it is being prosecuted in as low a key way as possible with strict adherence to the Hague Convention and subsequent regulations, and as much chivalry as the usages of war will allow. The British policy, almost a philosophy, of Minimum Violence has been shown to be the best even if it has occasionally resulted in apparently unnecessary casualties.

The principle of minimum violence taken to an extreme becomes non-violence, which usually manifests itself as civil disobedience. Civil disobedience is a common factor of urban insurrections, used as much as possible to discredit the security forces. However there are few cases of it being an important feature. The most famous example was that organised by Gandhi's Congress Party as a part of their struggle for Indian independence. Because of the war against the Japanese, during which the British-Indian army became the largest volunteer army the world has ever seen, it is difficult to estimate the efficacy of the use of non-violence. The Indian war effort and the promotion of Indian officers to senior positions ensured that there could be no return to the pre-war Raj totally regardless of the non-violence campaign. Non-violence did not sink deep into the Indian psyche, as was shown during partition when the resulting fighting caused many hundreds of thousands of deaths, probably over a million. Also upwards of fifteen million people were forced to abandon their homes and find refuge across the border in this horrifying and sudden reversion to something like primary warfare, as will be described in the next chapter. All this tragedy horrified Gandhi who did not believe he had any part in causing it. Five months after independence he was assassinated by a Hindu extremist who rejected his creed of tolerance.

Non-violence, as an insurrectionary method, can only work on the Indian model. That is a large number of people involved in civil disobedience against a government showing humanitarian restraint in its actions, and aware that it will soon be handing over power regardless of the outcome of the present confrontation. Providing the government is reasonably democratic then the ends of the non-violent campaign could be achieved just as easily by constitutional methods. As the government is less democratic so it helps to have a violent campaign lurking in the background so that the non-violent campaign will be taken more seriously.

The most well-known non-violent campaign held in Europe was the *Ruhrkampf*. This took place in 1923 when French forces occupied parts of the Ruhr basin to enforce the payment of war reparations that Germany was defaulting on. In the short term the non-violent campaign of civil disobedience, strikes and passive resistance was a failure. It resulted in over 140 German deaths, mostly as a result of exasperated French troops firing on crowds, and the French finally achieved the economic exploitation they aimed at. However in the longer view the French lost the moral high ground and lost the backing of the UK and the USA. Also they started the inflationary ball rolling that hurt everyone. In the long term both sides lost.

Non-violence works best by corrupting the security forces or rendering them helpless. The situation in India from racial and religious points of view was very sensitive, and the Indian soldiers came under immense social pressures. The British soldiers were few and overworked, and senior officers knew from the example of General Dyer that they would get very limited backing from the government if anything went wrong. The end result was that the Indian Congress Party gained a reputation for morality which some of its ruthless actions, particularly in Kashmir, did not dispel. This reputation was to serve India very well over the coming years.

In general non-violent protests, however moral, cannot stand against armed force. Alternatively they can, surprisingly often, be ignored.

Seizing and holding the Moral High Ground is important for practical reasons in the case of a long-running and inconclusive confrontation where the belligerents are dependent on financial aid from foreigners. This is because the foreign governments can only provide this support, on a long term basis, if their people approve, and the people will only approve if they regard the cause as being a moral one. The longer the confrontation lasts the more true this is. The obvious example of this is the Arab/Israeli confrontation, particularly in Gaza. Without the endless squabble over the moral high ground the origins of such confrontations would be forgotten and they would sink to the level of meaningless Capulet-Montague-type vendettas.

Finally an assessment must be made of the importance of morality in warfare, and this is that the perception of a just cause, or war aim, can result in people being more prepared to go to war, even though they concede that warfare is a wildly disproportionate reaction to the situation. A perceived lack of morality in the way the war is pursued will reduce their capacity for sticking it.

In the end this chapter has made little advance beyond the truth expressed in Livy's (Titus Livius, 59BC-17AD) aphorism '*Justum bellum quibus necessarium*'. War is just for those to whom it is necessary.

12

Inter-Communal War

As was stated in the introduction the preceding pages of this study have considered warfare as being secondary warfare. This chapter will consider a facet of warfare which can be regarded as approximating to primary warfare.

Inter-Communal War can occur when people of two races have been living alongside eachother, not integrated but in their own social units, villages or suburbs, they might even have been neighbours in the same street. They may have lived like this for generations, and if there had been any antagonism between the races it was halted by the central authority with its police and army. However if there were a sudden weakening of this central authority, and if there were an occurrence such as any kind of shortage or a trade recession, then the two communities would begin to view eachother with suspicion. If this situation lasted more than a short time then any little incident would be magnified by gossip and rumour until the two communities hated each other. When things are in this state any incident may spark a wave of 'tit-for-tat' violence.

Such violence would cause the people to form larger groups for self-defence. Small villages would be abandoned as their occupants flee to the safety of larger ones or towns. This will continue until either the minority is driven out of the country or the country is partitioned. The violence involved can be extensive and squalid.

Inter-Communal War has been one of the basic mechanisms of the great migrations. Villages of incoming Angles and Saxons may have been situated close to Celtic villages, and the occupants of the two villages may have even been on friendly terms for a while. But in the end they fought and the survivors of the weaker side were driven out and the stronger side occupied the deserted village. This kind of war, and primary war in general, is a method of resolving tensions that build up in peacetime. Therefore it is of great importance for the governments involved to understand these tensions and to do all they can to prevent them building up.

Inter-Communal War can be a long drawn-out process, or it can proceed fairly quickly as each side becomes more outraged at the other, and the restraining influence of the police is removed. This was tragically illustrated in India at the end of the British Raj.

The Second World War had undermined British rule. This resulted in a general degree of volatility which, with the certain knowledge that the British were leaving, made calm compromise between the Muslims and the Sikhs and Hindus impossible. It soon became obvious that British India would break up into Hindustan and East and West Pakistan. The lot of the Sikhs living in the future Pakistan, and the Muslims living on the other side of the border, was desperate. Each community was to be massacred and driven out. The British-Indian army and police fell apart as the British officers were withdrawn, and there was no-one to restrain the marauding bands. The result was murderous anarchy which lasted six weeks. The total death toll is unknowable but is usually put at a little over one million. The total number of migrants likewise is unknowable, but estimates have been as high as fifteen million. The bulk of these people lost everything they had and this represented a financial disaster in an inherently poor country.

A more recent, but equally horrifying, outbreak of Inter-Communal War was the killing of nearly a million Tutsis and Hutus in Rwanda and Burundi in the mid 1990s. The United Nations made no real attempt to stop this extreme cruelty, but it has to be admitted that there is often little that third parties can do. It was the British experience in Former Yugoslavia that once Inter-Communal War had started the only actions the army could take were to observe and to escort the fleeing migrants to comparative safety.

This type of warfare can sometimes show an amazing degree of social inversion. Amid the uncertainty and horror of the breakdown of public order, people who would normally be regarded as the lowest of the low, petty criminals and idlers, can arm themselves and suddenly seem like savours. They will initially act only against the minority but soon will give in to temptation and start looting indiscriminately and lording it over those who were once their betters. Social position and wealth, built up over the decades, can disappear in minutes and hopelessness will fuel emigration. Those with guns, of course, will be very reluctant to give them up.

In the modern age of widespread immigration many conflicts show some of the characteristics of Inter-Communal War. Two mentioned in this study have been Ireland and Cyprus, these resulting in partition. There are, though, other outcomes. One involves one of the parties being ground down until it is innocuous, as happened to the aboriginals in Australia and the red Indians in America. Another involves the expulsion of the losing party, as with the *pieds noirs* in Algeria, or arabs in the modern state of Israel. As with most of history, these events all seem to have been easily predictable, in retrospect.

An important aspect of Inter-Communal War is the lack of the government/army/people structure that is necessary for secondary warfare. In the fighting crowds each man, and each of the small number of women, was doing what he or she wanted to. It may be that some rabble rouser might have shrieked out the name of the next village to be attacked and this got the crowd in motion, but there was no real long term government. Inter-Communal War occurs only because of the lack of one.

The conditions for Inter-Communal War are immigration and the weakness of the central authority. Unfortunately this is not obvious to governments. Governments in general are reluctant to take determined steps to stop, or even substantially reduce, immigration. This is partly because they are not able to, partly because they do not want to appear callous and authoritarian, and partly because, in the short term, some immigration can seem to make economic sense. A country's economy will benefit if the workers' wages can be kept down. Immigrants will always work for lower wages than the indigenous population, so letting them in will keep wages down, and for this reason cause a good degree of antagonism.

In western countries the rate of immigration may seem to be slow and if the number of immigrants is small they can integrate, intermarry, and could, it is said, sometimes be beneficial to the host country. If, however, there is a large number of immigrants they will be much less likely to marry indigenous people as they have plenty of potential spouses among their own people. They will naturally tend to live close to each other and will take over whole suburbs. Doing this they will force out the original, inevitably working class, inhabitants, who will then move on to a non-immigrant area. If immigration continues then the country will ultimately consist of a patchwork of enclaves of different races. Their inhabitants might leave these enclaves to work, but after work will go straight back, and visiting another enclave, even in the same city, will be unthinkable. This process will continue until each enclave has more in common with similar enclaves in other cities than with the country in general, and organisations will spring up representing all the enclaves of each particular race. These organisations will start to replace the national government.

This process is taking place at a time when national warfare, which has the effect of uniting the country, is becoming less likely. It will be seen that when areas of people of different race and customs border each other there is always friction, and as each enclave is now listening to a different government the scene is set for inter-communal conflict which may be sparked by a trade recession or similar event. This scenario might seem far-fetched but its logic is irrefutable.

It could be said that, as immigration is a matter for individuals and not governments no matter how much they might try to control it, it can be looked at as being low level primary warfare. The difference between such actions in Europe and in Africa being that in Europe the original inhabitants are not massacred or driven out by force of arms.

The immigration considered above is that of poor people looking for a better life, but there is another kind. That is that of better off people buying property in another country. Such people are usually welcomed by the government of the host country as they are bringing money into the country, but it is possible to take the idea to what may be regarded as a ludicrous extreme when people of one country own a town in another. If that town were on the border with the buyers' country then the buyers' country could insist on the border being moved to encompass it. If this concept were joined to that of globalisation it is possible to postulate a major international company owning a factory, oil well or mine in an underdeveloped country. It could build or buy a town for its employees, and insist that its own laws, finances and even language applied in that town. The possibilities for friction are obvious.

The bad effects of immigration, and the resulting racial divide, will be hidden for a while by the government, but this itself can have a progressively bad effect on government/people relations. Via its police force it will try to compel the various races to co-exist through progressively coercive legislation. When the police are used in such a way, that is to enforce standards of behaviour rather than to prevent crime, then the expression 'Police State' becomes appropriate. Police states cause an increasing level of public discontent and, as the 20th Century demonstrated, do not last long. When they fall so do the controls on public behaviour and a great deal of pent up animosity will be revealed, resulting in pogroms, riots, ethnic cleansing and massacres, leading ultimately to partition as shown above. Yugoslavia is the obvious example.

If the two, or more, countries involved are adjacent then there may seem to be a case for setting up a super-national government. No matter how good this might sound in politicians' speeches, it will only compound the problem.

It can be seen that large scale immigration is a cause of conflict. What this will mean in the future is not easy to predict. For example the state of Florida now has a population the majority of which is Hispanic, but it is not clear if that fact will affect its position within the United States. What is clear is that governments must insist that immigrants assimilate as soon as possible and are loyal primarily to the national government. Otherwise the spectre of Primary Warfare will raise its head.

13

A Very Modern War

The Angolan Civil Wars

The previous chapters of this book have discussed war in terms of its various guises and aspects. This approach to the study of warfare might be necessary but is inevitably Eurocentric and, when considering the rest of the world, may have its limitations. A brief account is given in this chapter of the Angolan Civil Wars, and it will be seen that these wars can be considered in terms of any of the types of war so far covered, except nuclear. The conclusion drawn from this could reasonably be that there is little point in understanding classifications and types of war, but rather each war should be looked at individually on the basis of common sense. Such a conclusion would be hard to argue against.

One hazard of the Angolan wars is the vast number of sets of initials used to describe governments, political parties and armies, the language being usually Portuguese. This account will use the absolute minimum of these initials, so their use may not be always absolutely correct, just relatively so.

Angola was a part of the Portuguese colonial empire. Resistance against the colonial government started in 1961 with a general uprising. The Portuguese army put the urban rising down fairly easily, but could not totally pacify the countryside.

Retaining Angola and Mozambique cost Portugal a significant military effort which was maintained by conscript soldiers. This was a major factor resulting in the revolution, or military coup, of 1974, and this resulted in independence for Angola in 1975.

Although the Portuguese tried to set up a stable government, when they left things soon degenerated into chaos. The three major insurgent organisations, MPLA, UNITA and FNLA, were all supposed to be granted a share in the government, but in fact the MPLA seized power as soon as the Portuguese left. At the same time around half a million Portuguese settlers left Angola, leaving something of a power vacuum, and the scene was set for the insurgents to begin fighting each other. MPLA had Soviet backing and soon received assistance in the form of Soviet advisers and Cuban troops. The USSR was following its policy of extending its influence in Africa, and Cuba, being dependent on the USSR for manufactured goods and political support, was glad to help out. Also it may be suspected that Fidel Castro wanted to strut about on the world stage, a common failing among politicians.

The MPLA forces quickly drove FNLA northwards out of Angola, and FNLA became of little importance. UNITA troops were driven east and south, but managed to hold on, some of the areas they were in are covered with thick undergrowth and forests. As this was happening at the height of the Cold War, the USA started sending aid to UNITA, as did the Chinese. The South Africans, having more to lose, sent soldiers.

This resulted in a resurgence for UNITA, but in 1976 US aid was cut off. As a manifestation of the post-Vietnam syndrome the US government actually passed a law prohibiting the sending of aid to UNITA. Without this aid the South Africans could not sustain the campaign and their troops were withdrawn.

The UNITA forces had been almost at Luanda, the capital, but had to pull back eastwards. The bulk of the MPLA fighting seems to have been done by Cuban troops. Naturally UNITA remained a guerrilla army, whereas MPLA changed into a pale imitation of a Soviet force with more and more Angolans being trained as AFV crewmen. Even so no Cubans seem to have been withdrawn from Angola, but were redeployed from combat units into garrisons or support units.

The existence of the MPLA force, and the Soviet policy behind it, was a major worry to South Africa which started, initially on a small scale, supplying and training UNITA units. They also started to deploy combat units for the assault of entrenched garrisons which were too strong for the UNITA guerrillas. UNITA became steadily more effective, particularly in attacks on communications, which in Angola were long and vulnerable. South African troops also carried out raids into Angola to hit SWAPO bases. SWAPO was the organisation fighting the South Africans in Namibia. The upshot of this was that SWAPO troops started to fight against UNITA. UNITA also began to receive aid from Zaire which was reacting to a MPLA-backed invasion of one of its mineral rich provinces.

As UNITA became more successful so MPLA mounted a series of campaigns against it. They were all unsuccessful. The biggest and last of this series was in 1985. It was a disaster. The South African airforce hit the spearhead as did a South African heavy artillery unit. That halted it. UNITA troops and guerrillas hit the supply system. The Soviet and Cuban officers were helicoptered to safety, and the MPLA units broke up into a panic ridden retreat.

The Soviets decided to increase aid, and Castro needed a triumph to take his people's minds off their economic difficulties, so Cuban strength went up to around 65,000, which was roughly the same as UNITA. The upshot was a bigger and better offensive in 1987. MPLA attacked with four brigades in the front line, backed up by around 100 tanks and aerial superiority. Two South African battalions and a squadron of tanks undertook the greater part of the conventional mechanised fighting. They were very well supported by UNITA infantry, some of which were now regulars.

The resulting epic battle caused a rout for the MPLA troops. The survivors pulled back to a town called Cuito Cuanavale where the fighting bogged down. The Cubans, aided by the MPLA, tried to open an offensive on the Namibian border but were defeated by the South Africans. So a political settlement seemed best.

All the major participants were now tired of this war. Cuba had seen her troops defeated, in fact the Cuban commander was later arrested on Castro's orders, on what are generally agreed to be trumped up charges, and shot. The USSR, now under Gorbachev, was disengaging from its various foreign commitments, like Angola and Afghanistan. The USA and South Africa were finding it very expensive and were eager to quit. Consequently when the Soviets and Cubans agreed to go, the South Africans went. This left UNITA and MPLA to fight it out, which they did to a state of mutual exhaustion, generally favourable to UNITA. This war ended in 1991.

The truce, as it turned out to be, was short lived and, when UNITA refused to accept the results of an election, the Second Angolan Civil War started in 1992. The MPLA was now without foreign assistance and desperate. They employed three brigades of mercenary soldiers from Zaire, and they even called on a South African firm to supply a battalion of mercenary troops, which it did, to fight against the erstwhile South African allies, UNITA. International pressure forced the withdrawal of this unit after two years. The war degenerated towards primary warfare with mutual massacre, support from the population was maintained by terror and those with the largest conventional forces gained the upper hand. Both sides recruited soldiers, porters and women by surrounding villages and requisitioning the people they needed. It was common to have villages with people fighting on both sides, sometimes families had sons potentially fighting each other. The civilians lived in the terror of anarchy and the threat of starvation.

In the end the country was too large for either side to conquer it, communications were always too vulnerable to guerrilla action to support operations sustained enough to force a decision. The war ground to a halt in 1995. It ended generally favourably for MPLA, with a *de facto* partition of the country.

The Second Angolan Civil War was a humanitarian disaster, resulting in over 100,000 deaths. It was not conclusive and started again in 1997 when the government, MPLA, forces, benefiting from oil and diamond wealth, attacked UNITA again with some success. The leading spirit of UNITA, Jonas Savimbi, was killed in 2002 and then peace finally descended on Angola.

Aspects of the Angolan Wars

There are many remarkable aspects of the Angolan Wars. Probably the greatest is how they have been so ignored by the rest of the world. Another is the easy way they swung from vertical warfare, of the Angolans against the Portuguese Colonial Administration, to being a horizontal war between UNITA and MPLA. Similarly it oscillated between conventional and sub-conventional fighting.

Another remarkable aspect is the motivation of the warring sides. There were distinct racial motivations in the UNITA/MPLA struggle. UNITA was based on the Ovimbund, they were very black and proud of it. MPLA contained many Portuguese-Angolans, in fact Portuguese Angola was known as having no racial discrimination and consequently many mixed marriages. Consequently it is surprising that the main UNITA ally was South Africa which at that time was maintaining Apartheid. The racial nature of the fighting was reflected in the massacres of the Second Civil War, and subsequent fighting.

As a general point it must be noted how surprisingly durable the national borders in Africa have been. These borders grew, sometimes on a fairly random basis, out of the European colonisation process, and often showed little respect for racial boundaries. Despite this, and despite the many African wars since decolonisation, there has been no adjustment to national borders.

The USA was, most of the time, an ally of UNITA, which in itself is remarkable as UNITA was in theory a Maoist organisation. Conversely MPLA was dependent on diamond and oil sales to the USA. This resulted in the US government and oil companies speaking with different voices.

The greatest overall lesson of the Angolan Wars is that the side that can, and will, keep the largest conventional forces in the field longest will win in the end. This may seem simplistic, but it is true and often ignored.

There is a second lesson, but of a more limited and practical nature. That concerns the high quality of the South African heavy artillery, armoured vehicles and even desert boots. Because the apartheid regime was labouring under international sanctions it could not spend its military budget on expensive ships and planes, but could concentrate on lower-tech equipment that was really needed. Equipping for real war was the key to success.

Conclusion

Although this study has covered almost exclusively secondary warfare, the importance of primary warfare has been fully acknowledged. There is little doubt that primary warfare is always responsible for more deaths, suffering and destruction than secondary warfare and the possibility of a spread of primary warfare, usually in the form of inter-communal warfare, via the failure or bankruptcy of states, particularly in Africa, is very serious. It could be that in the future this trend will be seen as having been the most significant of the current age.

This study of secondary warfare has been based on the viewpoint that societies include the people, the government and the armed forces, a structure that has provided a protection against primary warfare, but encouraged secondary warfare. Further, that wars occur because at least one government decides that it wants to force another to change its behaviour in some way and it prepared to use force to do it.

This statement should indicate that war is the rational tool of policy, but even the most superficial glance at history shows that it is not. This is because either the politicians running the war, or the people supporting it, or both, depart from the purely rational. Further, it is true of horizontal, national, warfare and more so for vertical, internal, warfare where emotions can run higher and self-interest can be a greater motivation.

It has been seen that as the national structure of the world settles down and the more striking inequalities are ironed out, and progressively more states have nuclear weapons, so conventional warfare should become rarer. Also, as underdeveloped countries develop so primary warfare will become less common. Unfortunately it has also been seen that changes to the political structure of the world may occur, and these may not be entirely beneficial.

Over many years it has become plain that the interests of the people and the interests of the government can diverge, the more so the less representative the government is. A government's first loyalty is always to itself rather that to the people. It will do anything to retain power, and this will always be the case so long as there are career politicians, as these will always put their career before any kind of principle.

The antidote to this is more democracy. It is no coincidence that Switzerland is both the most democratic country in Europe and the most peaceful. It must be hoped that modern technology like the Internet, E-mail and mobile phones will assist the people to reassert their powers.

This view, though, is rather Eurocentric and may not be found to be totally appropriate to other parts of the world, for example, parts of the Muslim world. Also many countries have not yet reached the European level of political development, so nothing is conclusive.

Also the results of greater democracy can be unpredictable. In days past the authority of government was easily upheld by unrestricted violence and the threat of starvation. In modern times, in many if not most parts of the world, diplomatic pressure and world opinion have reduced governmental violence and improved methods of food preservation have made starvation less of a risk. These two factors have resulted in people that feel genuinely oppressed being prepared to riot. There have always been riots, and they have usually blown themselves out within a few days, as they did in Paris in 1968. The big change has come with mobile phones and the Internet, which is impossible to censor. Now riots, and a discontented population, can be directed by anyone who can broadcast sensible suggestions. The most important point is that the people are not under an alternative government, but each is acting individually. This was the situation during the *Intifada* of 1987-88, which proved impossible for the Israeli troops to handle. Successful rioting could well lead to the establishment of an alternative government, then to Vertical or Inter-Communal Warfare. Predicting future trends has never been more difficult, particularly as the Information Revolution may have dramatically altered the Government/people/army model.

Does all this mean that there will always be wars? Unfortunately it seems to. So long as the aims of the government differ from the wishes of the people there will be wars, and the treaty that concluded one war will quickly seem irrelevant in the ever changing world. History shows that properly set up nations with democratic governments do not have wars with similar countries. Also history has shown, by the experience of the USSR and Yugoslavia, the dangers of setting up super-national governments over what should be independent nations. But the vanity and ambitions of politicians must not be underestimated, and this is precisely what they will try to do.

So often a government will not defend the people because the politicians have no idea of the real world or ordinary people. Governments are upper and middle class organisations and have little understanding of the concerns of the working class. The main long term worry is immigration and it has been shown how this can result in Inter-Communal Warfare as the economic balance of the world shifts and populations inevitably grow. The future can be expected to become progressively volatile. Warfare, it seems, is endemic to the human race.

There will always be wars. So long as there are two men left who think there is something worth fighting about there will be wars. But when there are no longer those two men then, alas, humanity will have been reduced to the level of cattle, grazing placidly under the sun, till they roll over and die, of boredom.

THE END

APPENDIX 1

Some notes on the structure of the British Army written for a WRVS lady who ran a social club for soldiers. Though the tone of these notes is flippant their content is serious.

Notes on Basic Military Organisation

The Army is divided in two, roughly equally as far as numbers go. One part does the fighting, the other supports it.

The fighting part is made up of Battalions and Regiments. These terms are really interchangeable, the infantry says 'battalions', Armour and Artillery say 'regiments'.

The army is a hierarchical organisation. This means that there are lots and lots of people in charge. These break down into Commissioned Officers (Officers), Warrant Officers (WOs), and Non-Commissioned Officers (NCOs).

Officers: the top man in a battalion is the Colonel, actually he is only the Lieutenant Colonel, the Colonel is usually somebody royal but this can be ignored for day-to-day use.
Under him are Majors, Captains and Lieutenants, the lieutenants are both first and second lieutenants and overall are called Subalterns, they are referred to as 'Mr So-and-So', at least in cavalry regiments.
Officers are saluted and called 'Sir' by the rest. This is called 'Compliments'. Officers do this to other officers if they are senior to them, but not in the Officers Mess which should be on a Christian name basis.
Officers call the CO 'Colonel' when talking about matters internal to the regiment.
Officers, but nobody else, call the RSM 'Mr So-and-So'.
Each battalion has an Adjutant. He is usually a captain, and his job is to pass on the Colonel's orders, in fact to boss around the other officers. This makes him a Very Important Person.

WOs, these have the Queen's Warrant, as opposed to the Queen's Commission. They come in two ranks, WO1 and WO2 (WO one or two). There is a difference between rank and appointment:

WO1s may be the Regimental Sergeant Major (RSM), RQMS, or in the REME, ASM (Artificer Sgt Major, commonly known as 'Tiffy')
Interestingly, but of no real significance, the most senior of all WO1s is the RLC Conductor.
WO2s may be CSMs, SSMs, Pipe Majors, and probably several other things.

NCOs: sergeants (Sgts), Corporals (Cpls) and Lance Corporals (L/Cpls). Cpls and L/Cpls are called 'Full Screws' and 'Lance Jacks'.
There are also Staff Sergeants (also called Flag or Colour Sergeants). They are senior to Sgts, but below WOs. They do the little extra jobs like running stores, or training facilities, or really as little as possible.
Sgts and above are called Senior NCOs, Cpls are Junior NCOs.

There are also lots of people who are not in charge. These are called Junior Ranks (JRs or 'The Blokes'). They are mostly Privates, however they can have lots of other titles. In armour they are Troopers, in artillery they are Gunners, in the engineers they are Sappers, in the REME they are Craftsmen, in the Guards they are Guardsmen and in various regiments they may be Riflemen, Fusiliers, Kingsmen or even Queensmen. In the signals they are Signallers, they used to be Signalmen but that corps is now unisex!

Everyone who is not an officer used to be called an 'Other Rank' (OR). The army has been trying not to use this term since the 1960s and replace it by 'Soldiers', but I expect it lingers on.

A battalion, or regiment, commander is called the CO

(Commanding Officer). The officer commanding any other unit is called the OC (Officer Commanding). Don't ask me why!

A battalion is divided into companies (Coys) with rather over 100 blokes in each. Coys are divided into platoons with upwards of 40 blokes in each.
Similarly and armoured regiment is divided up into squadrons (Sqns), and these into four troops which are each of four tanks, 16 men.

A battalion is commanded by a Lt Col and the RSM (Regt Sgt Major)
A company   "   "   Major   "   CSM (Coy Sgt Major)
On tanks a sqn "   "   "   "   SSM (Sqn Sgt Major). The Major is referred to as the Squadron Leader (Squaddie)
A platoon, or troop is commanded by a Lieutenant and a Sgt.
Sub-divisions of platoons, sections, are commanded by Cpls, no officers at this level.

The Household Cavalry does not use the word 'Sergeant', they think it derives from the word 'Servant', so they say 'Corporal' instead, and have Regimental Corporal Majors etc, and a troop NCO (ie Sgt) is called a Corporal of Horse (CoH).

As you will have seen all units, ie regiments, squadrons and troops (battalions, companies and platoons) are commanded by two people, the Officer and the WO or NCO. The Officer is the senior of the two. It is said that the Officer commands looking outwards, ie to get the unit cooperating with other units, and the WO or NCO commands looking inwards to get the unit functioning correctly. Actually the system works well because it is not defined exactly who does what.

The officers and Sgts have their own separate messes where the single men live. These can be very plush (the messes that is). Troopers going into one must take off their berets. But then you will know this.

Corporals don't have a mess but single Cpls live in barracks with the Blokes. However they are entitled to a corporals' club. This is often called the Corporals' Mess just to confuse people. Corporals' messes, particularly on Friday and Saturday nights when the wives come in, can be quite violent places!

The JRs have the use of the NAAFI bar, ie Junior Ranks Club. Also when overseas each Sqn will set up its own bar where anyone can go.

Married men usually live in quarters. These men, their families and the quarters are referred to as 'Pads' (Personnel Army Dependants). They are usually regarded with jealousy, if not hostility, by the single men who believe that they skive fatigues and get generally better treatment. As the pads cannot eat in the cookhouse they spend dinner time in one of the messes or clubs, so tend to be useless in the afternoon.

Bigger and Better

Three or four battalions or regiments make up a Brigade. In order to make it sound more impressive we say 'Brigade Group'. It is commanded by a Brigadier. Two or three brigades make up a Division, commanded by a General. I very much doubt if there is a British division left in Germany.

At each level, battalion, brigade and division, there are supporting troops attached. On the lowest level a regiment will have cooks, medics, pay corps and REME. As the units get bigger so they will have more supporting troops, Signals, Intelligence corps, Logistics corps etc, etc.

227

The Others

There are also plenty of people employed outside this structure, they are the staff in stores depots, recruiting offices, tank ranges, training units, HQ and admin and dozens of other things. The officer commanding one of these establishments is usually called the 'Commandant'. Each of these establishments must be looked at as an individual case but the basic principles of military organisation apply.

APPENDIX 2

A copy of a small section of the 'Minimanual of the Irish Guerrilla'. This manual was produced by the Provisional IRA in 1971, crudely duplicated and widely distributed to republican sympathisers. The original of the copy was found in a house search in 1974.

It is of interest as it illustrates the hatred for the security forces that the insurgents try to foment. Also, throughout the manual there is no recognition of the fact that the majority of the population in Northern Ireland is Protestant and antagonistic to the IRA.

MINIMANUAL OF THE IRISH GUERILLA

A WAR OF

SOLDIERS OF THE OCCUPATION ARMY FOLLOW FREELY, AS CAREER, THE PROFESSION OF UNTIMELY DEATH. WE AS SOLDIERS OF THE PEOPLE'S REPUBLIC MUST MAKE THEM AWARE OF THIS AT EVERY OPPORTUNITY.

ATTRITION

Up to the moment of writing we have in general been on the defensive in this regard, killing only in retaliation. This policy has failed in that they – the killer war dogs - have not understood the purpose of it. The newspapers have also failed to grasp its significance

It is absolutely vital that from now on this policy be changed and that as soon as possible we go over to an unrelenting offensive, a war of attrition.

Bravado, whereby volunteers of the IRA have made suicidal stands against overwhelming odds (as in the beginning of

August 1971) must now cease. Their brave acts of self-sacrifice are worthy of the highest commendation; but they could have done so much more if they had deployed themselves in secure firing positions from which the attackers could have been shot down at much less risk to their indispensable lives.

For one man to hold down a platoon from cover is an extreme act of bravery. To do the same from a balcony in full view of the enemy is foolhardy. One IRA volunteer is worth the lives of 40 soldiers. This ration (sic) must be borne in mind in the future.

WHAT MAKES TOMMY TICK?

As a small group of republican soldiers keep station in defence of large areas against great numbers of enemy troops they may well ponder on the psychology and motivation of the forces opposing them.

(The myth of the "brave British Tommy" was , of course, exposed as a facile lie in the very first days of confrontation)

Well, the British soldier today is very like his Black and Tan forerunners in Ireland. In general he is cruel, vicious, stupid and a bully.

But do not underestimate him and his fellows for all that. Because if they get the upper hand, or sense a lack of resolution in their opponents, they will quickly take advantage of it.

Any prisoner taken by them will in a very short while be made aware of the bestiality inherent in their natures. In any guerilla-type war they tend to be very frightened men indeed and being so will vent their fear and frustration upon any one unfortunate enough to fall into their clutches – by beatings,

230

kickings, and even summary murder.

A well trained and resolute guerilla fighter will, if remaining cool under fire, always retain the advantage over soldier material such as this.

In an attack await a good target ... Aim your shots methodically ..... Use single shots in preference to bursts of machine gun fire ... This will make difficult the discovery of your position .... In the event of discovery continue quite calmly to aim your shots to kill.

<u>Shellfire is required to dislodge a sniper of courage who is well supplied with ammunition (vide G.P.O. Dublin 1916)</u>
No Tommy will advance against well aimed single shots from a trained marksman. The methodical killing of his comrades will quickly sap his morale and instead of moving forward his inclination will be to go the other way.

Fire groups of 2 men are the ideal for sniping operations such as the above: one to support the other from a different position – firing only when his comrades position is threatened or at obviously sure targets on which he is certain to strike home.

Some enemy troops, new to the war in Ulster, tend to treat it as a bit of a lark.

Bring reality home to these "new boys" quickly by inflicting casualties upon them as soon as they enter our streets. This will speedily dispel their "lark" attitude and will greatly help to turn their thoughts homewards with a consequent falling off of their usefulness as soldiers.

A parallel can be drawn between the British soldier and his counterpart in Civvy St, the skinhead. The latter kind of hooligans profess to hate all coloured man and make it their business, when out-numbering them, to beat them up and rob them.

They show a marked reticence, however, to approach the brawny negroes, preferring the easier targets supplied by the slight frames of Indians and Pakistanis. Furthermore, the readiness and ability of negroes to fight also has a marked bearing on the attitude of the skinhead to them.

So see the Tommies for the skinheads they are ..... Hit the bastards hard ..... Hit the bastards often ..... Get the Tommies tail between his legs and then drive your boot home to the third lacehole.

And as he leaves Ireland he will be full of love for you and will also have the greatest respect for you. For an English soldier is like a dog and will fawn upon those who master him and give him the occasional beating as a reminder of his condition.

APPENDIX 3

For many years military operations have been studied under a series of headings. These headings are called 'The Principles of War'. All armies use this approach, though the list of principles varies slightly from one army to another. Those given here are current in the British Army, and are copied from the manual 'Design for Military Operations – The British Doctrine', published in 1989.

Military operations must be studied and techniques mastered, but the words of the Duke of Wellington must never be forgotten when he said that generalship was '*common sense and attention to detail*', and to illustrate his meaning a paragraph from the Field Service Regulations, 1924, has been added.

The Principles of War

Selection and Maintenance of Aim

In the conduct of war, and therefore in all military activity, it is essential to select and define the aims clearly. The ultimate aim may be absolute, the overthrow of a hostile government, or more limited, the recovery of occupied territory. Within this strategic directive, a commander may have several courses of action open, each of which would fulfil the aim. The selection of the best course will lead to the mission and outline plan being issued, the mission being a statement of the aim and its purpose. The aim passed on to subordinate commanders may be precise or expressed in broader terms - for example, for a pursuit. It must nevertheless be unambiguous and attainable with the forces available. Once decided the aim must be circulated as widely as security allows so that all direct their efforts the achieve the aim.

Maintenance of Morale

Because success in war depends as much on moral as

physical factors, morale is probably the single most important element of war. High morale fosters the offensive spirit and the will to win. It will inspire an army from the highest to the lowest ranks. Although primarily a moral aspect it is sensitive to material conditions and a commander should look after the well-being of his men.

Offensive Action

Offensive action is the chief means open to a commander to influence the outcome of a campaign or a battle. It confers the initiative on the attacker, giving him the freedom of action necessary to secure a decision. A successful defence must be followed by offensive action if it is to achieve a decisive result. Offensive action embodies a state of mind which breeds the determination to gain and hold the initiative: it is essential for the creation of confidence and to establish an ascendancy over the enemy, and thus has an effect on morale.

Surprise

The potency of surprise as a psychological weapon at all levels should not be underestimated. It causes confusion and paralysis in the enemy's chain of command and destroys the cohesion and morale of his troops.

Concentration of Force

Military success will normally result from the concentration of superior force at the decisive time and place. This does not preclude dispersion which may be valuable for the purpose of deception and avoiding discovery and attack. Rapid concentration and dispersion depend on good communications and an efficient traffic control system. They also depend on balance, the essence of the next two principles.

Economy of Effort

The corollary of concentration of force is economy of effort. It is impossible to be strong everywhere and if decisive strength is to be concentrated at the critical time and place there must be no wasteful expenditure of effort where it cannot significantly affect the issue. In order to gain a substantial advantage a commander will have to take a calculated risk in a less vital area. The application of this principle may be summed up as planning for a balanced deployment combined with a prudent allocation of resources strictly related to the aim.

Security

A degree of security by physical protection and information denial is essential to all military operations. Security should enable friendly forces to achieve their objectives despite the enemy's interference. Active measures include the defence of bases and entry points, a favourable air situation, flank protection and maintenance of adequate reserves. The principles of concentration of force, economy of effort and security are all closely inter-related.

Flexibility

> "*No plan of operations can look with any certainty beyond the first meeting with the major forces of the enemy. The commander is compelled....to reach decisions on the basis of situations which cannot be predicted*"
>
> General Field Marshal von Moltke

Although the aim may not alter, a commander will be required to exercise judgement and flexibility in modifying his plans to meet changed circumstances, taking advantage of fleeting chances or shifting a point of emphasis. Flexibility depends upon the mental component of openness of mind on the one hand, and simple plans which can easily be modified on the other. A balanced reserve is a prerequisite for tactical or operational flexibility.

Co-operation

Co-operation is based on team spirit and training, and entails the co-ordination of the activities of all Arms, of the Services and of Allies, for the optimum combined effort. Goodwill, a common aim, a clear division of responsibilities and understanding of the capabilities and limitations of others are essential for co-operation

Administration

Sound administration is a prerequisite for the success of any operation. Logistic considerations are often the deciding factor in assessing the feasibility of an operation. A clear appreciation of logistic constraints is as important to a commander as his ability to make a sound estimate of the operational situation. No tactical plan can succeed without administrative support commensurate with the aim of the operation: it follows that a commander must have a degree of control over the administrative plan proportionate to the degree of his responsibility for the operation. Scarce resources must be controlled at a high level: the administrative organization must be flexible enough to react to changes in the situation with the most economic use of the available resources.

Field Service Regulations, Part II (1924), I.i(2)

Success in war depends more on moral than on physical qualities. Skill cannot compensate for want of courage, energy, and determination; but even high moral qualities may not avail without careful preparation and skilful direction. The development of the necessary moral qualities is, therefore, the first of the objects to be attained; the next are organisation and discipline, which enable those qualities to be controlled and used when required. A further essential is skill in applying the power which the attainment of these objects confers on the troops. The fundamental principles of war are neither very numerous nor in themselves very abstruse, but the application of them is difficult and cannot be made subject to rules. The correct application of principles to circumstances is the outcome of sound military knowledge, built up by study and practice until it has become an instinct.

Bibliographic Essay

It will have been noticed that I have not given references in this book. This is because I have been seriously studying war for nearly 50 years and I can no longer remember the source of some of my opinions and knowledge. To try to balance this lack of references I will recommend in this essay some books that I have found helpful, and which, to me, stand out amid the vast plethora of military books now available.

Of this plethora a distinct genre covers the history of the art of war. This subject is fascinating and the reader can derive immense pleasure from such books, but I'm bound to say that I do not find such books to be a great help in understanding modern war. Of these books I particularly like 'A History of War' by Field Marshal Montgomery, and 'War in the Modern World', by Theodore Ropp, but I imagine that there are many more just as good. Such books usually stop at 1945, the best summary of post-1945 war is 'War since 1945', by Jeremy Black.

The basis of warfare is politics and the *va-et-vient* of empires. Few books can provide more than good quality newspapers can over a number of years, but among those that can is 'The Rise and Fall of the Great Powers', by Paul Kennedy. His book of essays, 'Strategy and Diplomacy', is also well worth reading.

Practical aspects of running armies and wars are covered in 'How to Make War' by James F Dunnigan, which despite its almost childish title is full of common sense. The soldier's experience of war is covered in 'Firing Line', by Richard Holmes, and 'The Sharp End of War', by John Ellis, both good books, the latter restricting itself to the Second World War.

For conventional warfare the best introduction to armour is 'Tank Warfare', by Kenneth Macksey, even though it really ends in 1945. 'Razor's Edge', a history of the Falklands War by Hugh Bicheno, is good on practicalities and horrors of war.

There was a boom in books about Communist Revolutionary War in the 1960s, most of those I read were poor, but 'Revolutionary Guerrilla Warfare', by Geoffrey Fairbairn, stood out. Also 'The Indo-China War', by Edgar O'Ballance, has a good chapter on the subject, even if the author's political bias is a bit too obvious. 'On Protracted War', one of the red books by Chairman Mao, is worth reading.

'Terrorism' by Charles Townsend is the best book on the subject, it is one of the 'Very Short Introduction' series by OUP. That author has also written one of the standard books on the Anglo-Irish War, 'The British Campaign in Ireland, 1919-1921'. Peter Hart, writing on the same subject, has stirred up huge controversy with 'The IRA at War' and 'The IRA & its Enemies', probably by showing how squalid such conflicts are. The IRA in general is well covered in 'Fighting for Ireland?' by MLR Smith.

For the *Coup d'état* read 'How to Stage a Military Coup', by David Hebditch and Ken Connor. It is an unusual and entertaining book, but contains much good sense.

All books mentioned, of course, will have their own references and bibliographies, and the enquirer will soon become familiar with the literature available.

www.ingramcontent.com/pod-product-compliance
Lightning Source LLC
Chambersburg PA
CBHW030822090426
42737CB00009B/840